Self-Help for Narcissism

CRAFTED BY SKRIUWER

Copyright © 2024 by Skriuwer.

All rights reserved. No part of this book may be used or reproduced in any form whatsoever without written permission except in the case of brief quotations in critical articles or reviews.

For more information, contact : **kontakt@skriuwer.com** (www.skriuwer.com)

TABLE OF CONTENTS

CHAPTER 1: UNDERSTANDING NARCISSISM

- What narcissism means and why it matters
- Signs that point to harmful self-focus
- Effects on relationships and personal growth

CHAPTER 2: EARLY INFLUENCES ON SELF-FOCUS

- How childhood and family shape our view of ourselves
- Being overpraised or undervalued and its lasting effects
- Recognizing early signs of self-focused tendencies

CHAPTER 3: SPOTTING PROBLEM BEHAVIORS

- Common daily habits that reveal narcissistic traits
- Ways self-centered actions harm friendships and careers
- Learning to spot warning signals in your own behavior

CHAPTER 4: REDUCING SELF-CENTERED HABITS

- Practical steps to shift attention away from yourself
- The role of honest self-reflection
- Building healthier, more thoughtful routines

CHAPTER 5: LEARNING ABOUT EMPATHY

- Why caring about others' feelings is key
- Differences between sympathy and empathy
- Blocking factors that prevent showing genuine concern

CHAPTER 6: HELPFUL METHODS TO SHOW EMPATHY

- *Listening deeply and asking real questions*
- *Being present in conversations*
- *Kindness in action: small gestures with big impact*

CHAPTER 7: STEPS FOR INNER PEACE

- *Practices that calm the mind and reduce anxiety*
- *Slow breathing, gentle movements, and mindful breaks*
- *Balancing self-acceptance with healthy ambition*

CHAPTER 8: DEALING WITH ANGER AND PRESSURE

- *Recognizing triggers for frustration*
- *Constructive ways to cope with stress*
- *Turning difficult emotions into motivation for growth*

CHAPTER 9: BUILDING GOOD BOUNDARIES

- *Why personal limits matter for emotional health*
- *Saying "no" without guilt*
- *Respecting the boundaries of others while protecting your own*

CHAPTER 10: HANDLING GUILT

- *Differences between helpful and harmful guilt*
- *Overcoming self-blame and shame*
- *Making amends and then letting go*

CHAPTER 11: HEALTHY SELF-WORTH

- *Seeing your own value without ignoring your flaws*
- *Avoiding extremes of arrogance and self-hate*
- *Simple ways to build a balanced view of yourself*

CHAPTER 12: FOCUSING ON KINDNESS

- *Showing genuine care in day-to-day life*
- *Avoiding people-pleasing while still being considerate*
- *Being kind to yourself and others in small, steady ways*

CHAPTER 13: RELEASING HARMFUL THOUGHTS

- *Identifying common negative thinking patterns*
- *Mindful techniques to let go of worries and fears*
- *Reframing events to break out of old cycles*

CHAPTER 14: IMPROVING CONNECTIONS

- *Strengthening bonds with friends, family, and coworkers*
- *Practices for deeper conversations and trust*
- *Repairing damaged relationships with empathy*

CHAPTER 15: RESPONDING TO CRITICISM

- *Staying calm when faced with negative feedback*
- *Distinguishing helpful advice from mean remarks*
- *Turning critiques into learning experiences*

CHAPTER 16: LOOKING PAST YOUR OWN NEEDS

- *Why it helps to consider others' perspectives*
- *Practical ways to become less self-focused*
- *Building a shared sense of respect in relationships*

CHAPTER 17: EMPATHY IN DAILY LIFE

- Turning caring actions into everyday habits
- Adapting empathy to different personalities
- Supporting strangers, coworkers, and loved ones

CHAPTER 18: KEEPING A BALANCED MIND

- Maintaining emotional stability during stress
- Grounding techniques for anxiety
- Staying realistic about both success and failure

CHAPTER 19: MENDING EMOTIONAL WOUNDS

- Recognizing hidden hurts from the past
- Methods for releasing old anger or sadness
- Finding closure and rebuilding trust

CHAPTER 20: LONG-TERM POSITIVE CHANGE

- Integrating empathy, inner peace, and caring into everyday life
- Overcoming setbacks and sustaining new habits
- Living free from harmful self-focus and enjoying stronger connections

Chapter 1: Understanding Narcissism

Narcissism is a term that many people have heard, but not everyone knows what it truly means. It is often used to describe someone who talks about themselves too much, or someone who is seen as selfish or self-centered. Yet, the idea behind narcissism goes deeper than that. It can affect how a person thinks, behaves, and interacts with others. It can shape how they feel about themselves and the world around them. To better understand narcissism, it helps to look at what it is, what causes it, how it shows up, and the impact it can have on people.

It might be easier to think of narcissism as a focus on the self that goes beyond what is considered healthy. Most people have times when they want attention or when they feel proud of what they have done. That is normal. But a person who struggles with high levels of self-focus might place themselves above others in a way that hurts relationships. This problem can become bigger over time if it is not addressed.

A person with strong narcissistic tendencies might want praise from others. They might also think they are better than everyone else or feel entitled to special treatment. Because of this, they might not spend much time caring about how others feel. They could put their own wants first in almost every case. When this happens, it can lead to issues with friends, family, and even with themselves.

Below are several ideas about narcissism that can help you see it more clearly:

Narcissism as Part of Our Self-Image
Our self-image is how we view ourselves and how we believe others view us. For a person with a healthier sense of self, they know they have strengths and weaknesses. They understand they are not perfect, but they can still like themselves. Meanwhile, someone with strong narcissistic traits might feel they have few or no flaws. They might want constant praise to feel good about themselves.

Focus on Appearance or Social Image
Some people think of narcissism as an interest in looking good on the outside. Indeed, someone who struggles with narcissism might talk a lot about their looks, how much money they make, or other status symbols. They might also spend a lot of time managing their reputation, so that people see them in a bright light. This does not mean everyone who cares about how they look is a

narcissist. But the difference is in how much importance they place on being seen as special above all else.

Demanding Attention
Individuals who have high levels of narcissistic traits might seek attention in obvious or subtle ways. They may fish for compliments, or they may talk only about their achievements. In group situations, they could take over conversations to make sure everyone sees them as smart or unique. When they do not receive attention, they can feel upset or act out in different ways.

Lack of Empathy
One important sign of strong narcissistic traits is a lack of empathy. This means the person might have trouble understanding or caring about how others feel. They may not pause to think about the pain or frustration of others. This lack of empathy can create distance in relationships, as other people might feel ignored or unvalued.

Feeling Entitled
Entitlement is the belief that you deserve special treatment. A person with narcissistic tendencies might assume they are owed something, such as a better seat in a theater, or special favors at work. They can become upset or angry if they do not receive this special treatment. This sense of entitlement can cause conflict with others, who might see it as unfair or unreasonable.

How Narcissism Develops
The roots of narcissism can begin in a person's background, but it can also be influenced by life events. Sometimes, children who are overly praised or overly criticized may grow up feeling the world revolves around them, or that their needs are always the most important. Other times, it could be a defense against feeling unimportant or overlooked. Some people may learn narcissistic traits from family members who also focused too much on themselves.

Why It Matters to Understand Narcissism
Narcissism can cause many difficulties for the person who has it and for the people around them. If someone often seeks attention, or always tries to show themselves as the best, it can push people away. Friends or family may not feel listened to. Co-workers may feel overshadowed or unappreciated. In the long run, this can lead to loneliness and stress for the person showing these traits.

Mild vs. Strong Traits

There is a difference between someone who shows a few self-focused traits and someone who might be diagnosed with Narcissistic Personality Disorder. If a person is simply proud of their achievements and talks about them sometimes, that alone is not a cause for concern. But if someone displays a persistent need for praise, a lack of empathy, and an ongoing sense of being special above others, it may indicate a deeper issue.

Narcissism Across Cultures

Different cultures have unique ways of seeing self-focus. In some places, it may be normal to talk about personal successes. In others, doing so might be seen as rude or boastful. This does not mean narcissism is only present in certain cultures, but it can appear in different ways. A person's culture, family background, and social environment can all influence how they show self-focus.

Common Misunderstandings

Many people think of a narcissist as someone who just loves to look in the mirror. While that might be part of it, narcissism is more complex. Some individuals might appear outgoing and confident, but they could also be quite insecure. They may use bragging or seeking praise as a way to cope with deep worries about themselves. Others might not be flashy but could still have a sense of superiority over others.

The Importance of Openness to Growth

Understanding narcissism is the first step to changing harmful behaviors and improving one's well-being. People who recognize their own self-focused tendencies can learn new ways to think about themselves and how they relate to others. By being open to growth, they may learn to see others more, to hear their concerns, and to understand their feelings. This can lead to better bonds with friends, family, and co-workers.

Challenges in Recognizing Narcissism

It can be difficult for someone to see narcissistic tendencies in themselves. Often, the person believes their thoughts and actions are justified. They might even see themselves as a victim if they are not getting the attention they think they deserve. Because of this, friends or family members who want to help might face resistance.

Narcissism and Self-Esteem
It might sound strange, but narcissism can sometimes hide low self-esteem. A person might feel shaky about their value, so they build up a grand sense of self to protect themselves from shame or doubt. This is why they might lash out at even mild criticism—because it chips away at their fragile self-image. Recognizing that low self-esteem can be hidden behind narcissism can help in treating these issues.

The Role of Honesty and Insight
Growth begins when a person becomes honest with themselves. If someone thinks they might have some narcissistic traits, being open about it is key. Instead of denying it, they can take small steps to see how their actions affect others. This might mean listening more in conversations, asking sincere questions about others, or checking themselves when they start to boast.

Possible Effects on Daily Life
Narcissism can shape many parts of a person's day-to-day routine. For example, they might have trouble waiting in line, feeling annoyed because they believe they should go first. At work, they might ignore team efforts and only care about being seen as the best employee. At home, they could treat family members as if their needs are not as important. Over time, these behaviors can break down trust and closeness.

Influence on Emotions
People who struggle with narcissism can experience big mood swings. They might feel really good when they receive praise, but crash into sadness or anger if they feel ignored. This leads to what some call a "roller coaster" emotional life, where happiness depends on how much attention they get. Learning about these patterns can help a person take control of their emotions.

Long-Term Consequences
Unchecked narcissism can lead to problems such as failed relationships, job loss, or isolation. Friends might walk away if they feel used or unheard. Romantic partners can become frustrated if they are always put second. Employers might lose patience if the narcissistic person does not respect team goals. Recognizing these risks may motivate some people to change.

Why Empathy and Inner Peace Matter
At the heart of this book is the aim to help a person move past a harmful pattern

of self-focus and find more empathy and calmness within themselves. Empathy allows us to bond with others, share in their feelings, and show kindness. Inner peace helps us feel stable and calm, even when we face stress. By combining these, a person can build happier and healthier relationships, both with themselves and with others.

Looking Ahead
This book will offer practical steps to become more aware of how self-focus might be damaging you or the people you care about. It will suggest ways to strengthen your ability to see others. It will also include ways to build a greater sense of calm and acceptance in everyday life. By breaking down each topic step by step, you can learn to let go of harmful habits and find a more balanced sense of self.

Summary of Main Points

- Narcissism involves an unhealthy focus on the self that can harm relationships.
- Common signs include seeking attention, having little empathy, and feeling entitled.
- It can be connected to a shaky sense of self-worth or past negative experiences.
- Recognizing these traits is the first step to making positive changes.
- Empathy and inner calm can help people move beyond harmful patterns and form better connections.

This chapter serves as a broad overview of the topic. It sets the stage for a deeper look into how narcissism can grow from early influences, how to spot it in daily actions, and how to replace unhealthy patterns with positive ones. The chapters ahead will address more specific problems and give ideas on how to handle them.

When you finish reading all the chapters, you will have a clearer view of what narcissism is, where it might come from, and what steps you can take to care more about others while also finding a sense of calm within yourself.

Chapter 2: Early Influences on Self-Focus

Many traits can be traced back to childhood. From a young age, we learn how to see ourselves, how to see others, and what behaviors are acceptable or rewarded. In some families, a child might be given too much praise, leading them to think they can do no wrong. In other families, a child might be ignored or criticized, causing them to seek ways to feel special. This chapter explores how those early experiences can shape a person's sense of self-focus and possibly contribute to narcissistic tendencies.

How Families Shape Our View of Ourselves

Families are our first teachers. Before we go to school or make friends, our parents or caregivers influence our sense of self. If a parent praises a child for every little thing, even if the child did not put in effort, the child might grow to expect constant applause. On the other hand, if a parent never shows warmth or acceptance, the child might feel empty and crave attention. This could later show up as self-focused behavior, in which the person tries to fill that emptiness by seeking admiration from others.

The Effects of Being Overpraised

It might sound strange to think that praising a child can have negative effects, but it depends on how the praise is given. Overpraising can send the message that the child is always correct or always special. This can create unrealistic expectations. The child might start to believe that everything they do must be admired. When they step into the real world and do not receive that same level of praise, they might become frustrated. They may continue to seek that feeling of being the "star," even if it means ignoring others.

The Effects of Being Undervalued

Another side of the story is when a child feels overlooked or treated as if they are not enough. If parents are too busy to notice them, or if they speak harshly to them on a daily basis, the child might learn to see themselves as unimportant. Later in life, that child may try to make up for these feelings by building a grand sense of self. They could exaggerate their achievements, demand attention, or take any criticism as a deep wound. This approach can become a coping style to cover up years of feeling unimportant.

Modeling Behavior from Parents
Children learn by copying what they see. If a parent constantly brags, or looks down on others, a child might pick up these habits. If a child sees a parent dismiss others' feelings, they may learn that other people's emotions are not that important. Over time, this can create adults who find it normal to focus mostly on themselves. They might not even see anything wrong with it, because it is what they observed growing up.

Siblings and Birth Order
In some families, the focus on one child can be stronger if that child is the oldest or the youngest. Parents might shower the youngest child with attention, for instance, and fail to teach them important lessons about sharing the spotlight. Or, the oldest child might feel a pressure to excel and become the "golden" child in the family's eyes. These sibling dynamics can lead to different forms of self-focus, either from too much attention or from too much pressure.

Early School Experiences
When a child starts school, they encounter teachers, classmates, and challenges that shape their behavior. A child who easily excels in school might become used to praise and feel that they are better than others. A child who struggles might feel overshadowed, which could lead them to find other ways to stand out. They might start showing off, talking loudly, or even becoming the class clown to gain the attention they do not get through good grades.

Friendships in Childhood
Childhood friendships also matter. If a child feels they can only be included by being the loudest or by acting in a self-centered way, they may keep doing that. If they get attention for acting out, they might continue those patterns. On the other hand, if a child has friends who support each other, they might develop empathy and learn to share and listen.

Small Traumas and Lasting Effects
Sometimes, events that seem small can have long-term effects. A child who is laughed at in front of a crowd might try to avoid ever looking weak again. They might build a false sense of self where they are always "on top." This is one way self-focus can become a guard against feeling hurt. Even though it can keep the person feeling safe in the short term, it can create walls between them and others in the long run.

Peer Pressure and Popularity

During teenage years, popularity can become very important. Teenagers might worry about whether they fit in or are admired. Some teens might shape their identity around being seen as better, more stylish, or more skilled. This can include putting down others or only focusing on their own achievements. These habits can persist into adulthood if they are not recognized and changed.

Social Messages

Media and society can also influence self-focus. For example, some ads tell us that we should always focus on what we want or that we deserve to have it all. While having goals is fine, constant messages about being on top can encourage people to put themselves before everyone else. Children and teens who consume this content might believe that self-focus is the key to success.

When Self-Focus Becomes Self-Defense

For some, a self-centered approach is a defense mechanism. If a child grows up feeling insecure or unsafe, they may develop a behavior pattern of putting themselves first at all costs. They might think, "If I don't look out for me, no one will." This can become a habit so strong that they have trouble trusting people. As a result, they may ignore other people's needs and feelings to stay safe.

Identifying Early Signs of Self-Focus

Parents, teachers, or guardians might notice early signs of self-focus in a child who constantly interrupts others or who always wants to be in charge during games. Although these behaviors can be normal in small doses, if they are extreme or do not improve over time, it might mean the child needs guidance. Gentle conversations, setting boundaries, and showing empathy in the home can help them see the value of caring about others.

Breaking the Cycle

Some families carry patterns of self-focus from one generation to the next. If a parent did not learn empathy in childhood, they might pass on the same behaviors to their children. Breaking this cycle can happen when someone decides to change. They might seek counseling, read self-help materials, or talk to trusted people. By taking such steps, they can learn to see beyond themselves and avoid passing the same harmful habits on to the next generation.

Early Signs vs. Adult Responsibility

While childhood experiences shape a person, it does not mean that change is impossible or that someone is locked into these traits forever. Adults have the chance to rethink what they learned as children. They can ask, "Why do I feel the need to be praised all the time? Why do I ignore other people's feelings?" By reflecting on these questions, they can begin to adjust their behavior. This can lead to healthier relationships and a stronger sense of well-being.

Why Understanding These Influences Is Important

By realizing how self-focus might have started, a person can better understand their own actions in the present. It helps to see that maybe there was a reason they became so focused on themselves. Maybe they felt unseen or unsure. Knowing that does not excuse harmful behavior, but it does open the door to forgive oneself and move forward. It also helps them see that they have the power to improve their habits.

Practical Ways to Address Early Influences

- **Reflect on Your Childhood:** Think about how your parents or caregivers acted. Did they often brag? Did they never offer kindness or praise? Did they do so too much? Recognizing patterns is the first step.
- **Talk to Siblings or Others Who Knew You Then:** They may share memories or insights about your childhood that you had forgotten.
- **Look for Links to Your Current Behavior:** If you find yourself always seeking approval, can you link that to how you felt as a child? Does it stem from being ignored or always cheered on in an unbalanced way?
- **Seek Professional Help if Needed:** A counselor can help you explore childhood experiences and guide you in forming healthier habits.

The Role of Self-Awareness

Self-awareness means being mindful of your thoughts, feelings, and actions. Developing self-awareness helps you spot when you might be acting out of old childhood patterns. For instance, if you find yourself insisting that a coworker do things your way, pause and ask if this relates to a time in your childhood when you felt powerless. Self-awareness can help stop harmful patterns in their tracks.

Building Empathy Early On

Ideally, children learn empathy from adults who show it. They learn to listen and care about their friends or siblings. If a child does not learn empathy young, they can still learn it as adults. It might take practice, such as asking others about their day and truly listening, or noticing when someone is sad and offering a kind word. This skill, once learned, can counter self-focused behavior.

Replacing Old Patterns with Better Habits
If a child grew up in an environment that encouraged them to brag or dismiss others, they can choose a different approach in adulthood. They can form a habit of letting others speak first in a conversation or offering help without expecting praise. Each time they do this, they create a new pattern in their mind, moving away from the old self-focused path and onto a more caring one.

Hope for Positive Growth
Many people who were raised in environments that shaped self-focused behaviors manage to change their outlook. They discover that real connection with others brings deeper satisfaction than always trying to be the center of attention. They learn that empathy allows them to connect with people in a genuine way. This can lead to better friendships, stronger family bonds, and a sense of calm.

Summary of Main Points

- Childhood experiences can greatly shape whether a person grows up with strong self-focused traits.
- Overpraising can lead a child to expect constant admiration. Being undervalued can make a child seek recognition later in life.
- Observing parents or other adults who put themselves first can teach a child to do the same.
- Early signs of self-focus can sometimes be turned around with patience, honest reflection, and empathy-building steps.
- Understanding why these traits developed does not excuse harmful behavior, but it can guide a person toward making better choices as an adult.

When we look at our early backgrounds with clear eyes, we often see how habits were formed. This awareness is helpful in letting go of patterns that do not serve us. It also lays the groundwork for a healthier sense of self, where we can value who we are while also caring about others. In the following chapters, you will learn how to spot problem behaviors in daily life, as well as how to break free from them. You will also find out how learning empathy can be the key to improving your connections and creating a more peaceful inner life.

Chapter 3: Spotting Problem Behaviors

People often notice self-focused behaviors in others more easily than they see them in themselves. This can be because we do not always step back and look at our own actions. In this chapter, we will talk about how to spot specific behaviors that might point to a harmful level of self-focus. We will explore examples in daily life, relationships, and work or school situations. By learning to recognize problem behaviors, we gain the power to address them before they cause more harm.

Not Listening When Others Speak
A major sign of problem behavior is failing to listen when others share their thoughts. For example, if someone interrupts regularly or changes the topic back to themselves, this can show too much self-focus. We might think our story or opinion is more important, so we hardly pay attention to what the other person is saying. Over time, people who feel unheard might begin to distance themselves.

    a. **What It Looks Like:**
        i. Interrupting someone mid-sentence
        ii. Checking your phone or looking bored when they speak
        iii. Only waiting for your turn to talk without truly hearing what the other person is saying
    b. **Why It Happens:**
        i. You might be excited to share your own thoughts
        ii. You might feel your viewpoint is more valuable
    c. **Impact on Others:**
        i. They can feel dismissed or unimportant
        ii. They might not want to share again if they think you do not care

Monopolizing Conversations
Another clear sign is monopolizing discussions. This involves talking a lot about personal stories, achievements, or opinions and leaving little room for others to speak. It might seem harmless, but it prevents real exchange. Some people might

talk a lot because they think their ideas must be heard, or they believe they can do no wrong. Others might do it without realizing they are shutting people out.

    d. **What It Looks Like:**
        i. Speaking much longer than anyone else
        ii. Telling personal stories that do not involve or interest the group
        iii. Cutting others off so you can keep going
    e. **Why It Happens:**
        i. You might feel that your knowledge or experiences are extra special
        ii. You could be used to getting attention and have not learned to share space
    f. **Impact on Others:**
        i. Others may feel their voices do not matter
        ii. Listeners could see you as arrogant or uncaring

Needing Constant Praise

Some individuals look for a steady stream of compliments or approval to feel okay. When that approval does not come, they might become angry or hurt. A strong need for praise can show a deeper issue with self-esteem. It might stem from times in life when the person did not feel valued, or it might come from being overpraised as a child. Regardless of the cause, the behavior can affect relationships.

- **What It Looks Like:**
  - Fishing for compliments ("Don't you think I did the best job?")
  - Becoming sad or upset if someone else gets praise
  - Bringing up achievements out of context to hear how great you are
- **Why It Happens:**
  - You may have a shaky sense of self-worth
  - You might believe you deserve constant admiration
- **Impact on Others:**
  - They can feel drained, as if they have to feed your need for praise
  - Genuine admiration can become forced or meaningless

Lack of Concern for Other People's Feelings

A big concern is when a person often fails to consider what others might be going through. They may say harsh things and brush off any sign of hurt from the other side. When people close to them feel ignored or mocked, relationships begin to suffer.

- **What It Looks Like:**
    - Not apologizing if you cause hurt
    - Saying mean things, then acting like it is not a big deal
    - Showing little interest in helping someone who is upset or in need
- **Why It Happens:**
    - A strong focus on your own wants can leave little room for understanding others
    - You might think the other person should "toughen up"
- **Impact on Others:**
    - They might feel unloved or unseen
    - They could pull away to protect themselves

Jealousy and Envy

Feeling jealous or envious is not unusual, but it becomes a problem if it leads to harmful actions. A self-focused person might become angry or annoyed when others are successful. They might try to take away from the achievements of others to feel better about themselves. This can weaken friendships and family ties.

- **What It Looks Like:**
    - Dismissing someone else's success by calling it "luck" or "easy"
    - Putting down the person who did well in order to feel superior
    - Criticizing or spreading rumors
- **Why It Happens:**
    - You may feel threatened by someone else's achievements
    - You might believe there is not enough praise to go around
- **Impact on Others:**
    - They feel hurt or betrayed
    - Their joyful moments are spoiled

Taking More Than Giving in Relationships
Healthy relationships require a balance of giving and receiving. Whether it is emotional support, time, or kindness, both sides should share in some way. A sign of problem behavior is if you regularly accept help or attention but do not return it. Over time, people might feel used or taken for granted.

- **What It Looks Like:**
    - Expecting others to adjust their schedules for you, but not doing the same for them
    - Asking for favors, money, or time without giving anything in return
    - Always leaning on others for comfort without showing concern for their troubles
- **Why It Happens:**
    - You might believe your needs are more important than theirs
    - You could assume it is their duty to help you
- **Impact on Others:**
    - They become tired of giving
    - They might pull away to avoid feeling exploited

Difficulty Accepting Responsibility
Another problem behavior is blaming others when things go wrong, even if you had a hand in the issue. Admitting mistakes can be hard for someone who is afraid of looking weak or imperfect. They might shift responsibility to a friend, co-worker, or family member to protect their self-image.

- **What It Looks Like:**
    - Making excuses for poor choices ("I was late because my friend made me wait," even if that is not true)
    - Ignoring your part in conflicts ("They're just too sensitive," rather than owning your unkind words)
    - Trying to rewrite events to avoid guilt
- **Why It Happens:**
    - Fear of appearing flawed
    - Desire to keep a perfect image
- **Impact on Others:**
    - They feel blamed for things they did not do

- It becomes hard to trust someone who never admits mistakes

Using People for Personal Gain

Sometimes, a highly self-focused person may see others primarily as a way to get what they want. They might act friendly or charming if it helps them move ahead. But once they have taken what they need, they could drop the person without a second thought.

- **What It Looks Like:**
  - Pretending to share interests just to form a connection that benefits you
  - Ending contact with someone the moment they can no longer help you
  - Manipulating or flattering people in power so they will promote or favor you
- **Why It Happens:**
  - Seeing relationships as a means to an end
  - Believing your desires outweigh the well-being of others
- **Impact on Others:**
  - They feel betrayed or used
  - It can destroy trust in future interactions

Mood Swings Based on External Approval

Sometimes, the self-focused person's mood will depend greatly on how others react to them. If they receive praise or compliments, they might feel good. If they experience criticism or feel overlooked, they can become angry or sad very fast. This pattern suggests that their sense of self-worth is dependent on outside feedback, which can be a sign of deeper challenges.

- **What It Looks Like:**
  - Feeling very excited and confident one minute, then hurt and upset the next
  - Relying on "likes" or comments on social media to feel okay
  - Having a hard time dealing with small criticisms
- **Why It Happens:**
  - Self-image might be fragile and needs constant support
  - Any slight can feel like a huge threat to your confidence
- **Impact on Others:**

- They might feel pressure to always be positive around you
- They can become tired of walking on eggshells

Emotional Outbursts Over Small Matters

A person with strong self-focused tendencies might have big emotional reactions to things that would not bother most people. If they do not get their way, they can lash out in anger or show extreme sadness. This might leave others feeling confused or worried.

- **What It Looks Like:**
    - Yelling or slamming doors when a small request is not met
    - Acting as if a minor disagreement is a huge offense
    - Threatening to end relationships or quit jobs over small disputes
- **Why It Happens:**
    - There may be an underlying fear of not being in control
    - Minor disappointments can feel like major insults
- **Impact on Others:**
    - They might fear telling you honest feedback
    - They could avoid you or stay silent to keep peace

Ignoring Social Norms or Rules

In social situations, most people learn unwritten rules: wait your turn, do not cut in line, or do not speak too loudly when others are resting. A self-focused person might ignore these norms, feeling they are above them. This disregard can cause tensions and show a lack of empathy for how actions affect others.

- **What It Looks Like:**
    - Cutting in front of others without shame
    - Talking loudly in quiet spaces as if the comfort of others does not matter
    - Leaving a mess in shared areas for others to clean
- **Why It Happens:**
    - Strong sense of entitlement
    - Not valuing the common good
- **Impact on Others:**
    - Creates frustration or even confrontation
    - Breaks trust or harmony in group settings

Trying to Control Others' Choices

A person might try to dictate what others wear, eat, or do for fun. They may insist that their partner or friend should act a certain way. Although giving advice can be kind, forcing opinions on others or mocking their choices can show self-centered thinking.

- **What It Looks Like:**
    - Telling a friend which hobbies they should have
    - Mocking a partner's clothing until they change to please you
    - Using guilt or manipulation to shape someone's behavior
- **Why It Happens:**
    - A feeling that your preferences are correct and must be followed
    - Using control to feel secure
- **Impact on Others:**
    - They lose confidence in their own decisions
    - They may fear telling you what they truly want

Dismissing Other People's Accomplishments

Sometimes, a person might act unimpressed or uninterested when someone else shares good news. Instead of showing support, they might change the subject or try to top the story with their own. This behavior can damage friendships and create a negative atmosphere.

- **What It Looks Like:**
    - Responding to someone else's happy moment with your own bigger "win"
    - Shrugging off a friend's achievement as "no big deal"
    - Withholding congratulations or polite remarks
- **Why It Happens:**
    - Not wanting others to feel special
    - Feeling threatened by another person's success
- **Impact on Others:**
    - They feel overshadowed
    - They become less likely to share accomplishments with you

Acting Differently Around People of Influence

A self-focused person might switch how they act based on who they think can help them. For instance, they may be overly polite and friendly to a boss or someone with status, but rude or dismissive toward a server or subordinate. This pattern shows a lack of genuine respect for people as individuals.

- **What It Looks Like:**
    - Praising or flattering the person in charge, but ignoring or insulting coworkers
    - Putting on a charming face when seeking a favor, but turning cold afterward
    - Only showing manners when there is a direct benefit
- **Why It Happens:**
    - Hoping to gain something from those in power
    - Believing that those with less power are not worth respect
- **Impact on Others:**
    - Creates an atmosphere of dishonesty
    - People feel hurt by the unequal treatment

Minimizing the Feelings of Those Close to You

In close relationships, empathy plays a big role. If a partner, child, or friend comes to you with a concern, they trust you to listen and care. A self-focused person might brush off or belittle the problem, perhaps by saying, "You're overreacting," or, "That's silly." This can break down trust and leave the other person feeling alone.

- **What It Looks Like:**
    - Rolling your eyes or acting bored when someone shares their worries
    - Laughing or mocking someone who is in distress
    - Telling them to "get over it" without offering support
- **Why It Happens:**
    - Lack of interest in other people's emotional well-being
    - Finding it hard to see beyond your own feelings
- **Impact on Others:**
    - They feel judged or hurt
    - It weakens emotional closeness

Not Learning from Mistakes

Everyone makes mistakes. But a self-focused person might ignore lessons from those mistakes if it means admitting they were wrong. They could repeat the same behavior, hurting others or themselves each time. This can stall personal growth.

- **What It Looks Like:**
    - Brushing off feedback that could help you improve
    - Arguing or getting angry when someone points out a recurring pattern
    - Continuing harmful behaviors despite warnings or past outcomes
- **Why It Happens:**
    - Denial of flaws
    - Need to maintain a faultless image
- **Impact on Others:**
    - They feel forced to deal with the same problems over and over
    - It can lead to anger and resentment in close relationships

Blocking Others from Expressing Their Needs

Sometimes, a person might make it so that no one else can speak up about what they want. They might do this by controlling a discussion or dismissing any desire that does not line up with their own. This can happen in group settings, like family gatherings or project teams.

- **What It Looks Like:**
    - Refusing to hear any plan but your own
    - Mocking or belittling other ideas
    - Shutting down someone who tries to voice a concern
- **Why It Happens:**
    - Belief that your plan is the only good plan
    - Feeling that others' needs are not important compared to yours
- **Impact on Others:**
    - They lose motivation to participate
    - They might stop sharing their ideas or feelings

Emphasizing Your Feelings Over Everyone Else's

Each of us has our own struggles. Yet a self-focused person may act as though their struggles are always the worst or most pressing. They could ignore the reality that others are dealing with their own tough times.

- **What It Looks Like:**
    - Telling a friend that their pain is "nothing" compared to yours
    - Making every conversation about your hardships
    - Getting upset if others do not drop everything to comfort you
- **Why It Happens:**

- Difficulty seeing the world from another person's point of view
    - Desire to keep the spotlight on yourself
- **Impact on Others:**
    - They feel their issues are not valid
    - They might stop sharing, leaving you with less insight into what they face

Focusing Too Much on Personal Gain in Group Work

Whether at school, on a sports team, or in a job, a self-focused person might only care about how the group's work affects their own success. They may not help teammates unless there is a direct benefit, and they may try to take credit for group achievements.

- **What It Looks Like:**
    - Volunteering only for tasks that get the most attention
    - Downplaying the contributions of others
    - Refusing to do "boring" but necessary work
- **Why It Happens:**
    - Seeking recognition and avoiding tasks that lack glory
    - Not seeing the value of teamwork for its own sake
- **Impact on Others:**
    - Team spirit is lost
    - Others might become frustrated or feel taken advantage of

Missing the Point of Shared Experiences

In group settings like family dinners or outings with friends, a self-focused person might treat the event as just another chance to talk about themselves. They do not pay attention to the shared connection or the interests of the group.

- **What It Looks Like:**
    - Tuning out any part of the conversation that does not center on you
    - Boasting about personal wins when the group is trying to bond
    - Leaving early if you are not the center of attention
- **Why It Happens:**
    - You may find little value in listening to others' stories or experiences
    - You might prefer environments where you can shine
- **Impact on Others:**

- They lose the sense of togetherness
  - They might not invite you next time

How to Start Noticing These Behaviors in Yourself
Recognizing these signs in yourself might not be easy. However, there are some ways to increase self-awareness:

- **Reflect After Conversations:** Ask yourself if you gave others a fair chance to speak. Did you focus only on your stories?
- **Observe Emotional Reactions:** Notice if you become upset when you do not receive praise. Ask why that triggers a strong emotion.
- **Listen to Feedback:** If trusted friends or family members say you talk about yourself too much, take time to consider their comments without getting defensive.
- **Track Your Thoughts:** Write down moments when you feel the need to prove yourself or get attention. Look for patterns over time.
- **Pause Before Speaking:** When in a group, try waiting a moment to let others add their ideas first. This gives them space and shows you value what they have to say.

Why Spotting These Behaviors Matters
If these problem behaviors go unnoticed, they can damage your relationships and overall well-being. You may end up lonely or struggle at work or school. However, when you see these signs, you can begin taking steps to fix them. Spotting the behaviors is the first move toward creating better habits and finding more calm and satisfaction in life.

Identifying problem behaviors does not mean you are a bad person. It just means there is room to improve. The next chapter will focus on methods you can use to reduce self-centered habits and change how you relate to others.

By learning to spot these red flags, you open the door to positive growth. You can choose to speak differently, listen more, and treat others with respect. Over time, these choices can lead to better connections with friends and family, stronger performance at work or school, and a deeper sense of calm inside yourself.

Chapter 4: Reducing Self-Centered Habits

Now that we have looked at the signs of harmful self-focus, the next step is to figure out how to reduce those habits. Changing these patterns can feel hard, but it is possible to do so with a clear plan, honest self-reflection, and steady effort. This chapter offers practical steps for shifting attention from yourself to others in healthy ways. By making these changes, you can improve how you interact with people and how you see yourself in the process.

Practice True Listening

Listening is more than just letting someone speak. It involves giving them your full attention and caring about what they say. True listening also means asking questions to understand better and avoiding the urge to turn the topic back to yourself.

- **How to Do It:**
    - Maintain eye contact and put aside your phone or distractions
    - Focus on their words, tone, and body language
    - Ask simple clarifying questions like, "How did that make you feel?"
    - Resist the urge to respond with your own stories right away
- **Why It Helps:**
    - It shows respect and value for the other person
    - It trains you to be more aware of others, reducing self-centered thinking

Keep Track of Speech Balance

In a conversation, notice if you are talking more than the other person. If you find yourself dominating, slow down and let them speak. This balance can also help you see if your conversation is fair.

- **Practical Tip:**
    - Use a simple check: "Have I asked the other person any questions about their life?"
    - If the answer is no, pause and invite them to share
- **Why It Helps:**

- It builds mutual trust and respect
- Others feel included, which makes interactions more positive

Set Limits on Boasting
It is normal to be proud of achievements, but constantly talking about them can drive people away. If you see a pattern of bragging or seeking praise, set a rule for yourself to limit how often you bring up these accomplishments.

- **How to Do It:**
  - Remind yourself that not every success needs to be announced
  - Try to let others share their successes before talking about yours
  - If you catch yourself bragging, gently shift focus to someone else's point of view
- **Why It Helps:**
  - Reduces the risk of appearing arrogant or uncaring
  - Encourages a more balanced view of your successes and others' successes

Learn Empathy Basics
Empathy is the ability to see and feel from another person's perspective. If you do not practice it much, you can start with simple steps.

- **Ways to Build Empathy:**
  - Watch movies or read books that explore a character's feelings
  - Ask people around you how they are doing, and truly listen to the answer
  - When someone shares a problem, say, "That must be hard," rather than dismissing it
- **Why It Helps:**
  - Encourages you to pay attention to others' emotional states
  - Reduces the habit of focusing only on yourself

Offer Help Without Expecting Anything
A key part of reducing self-centered behavior is giving freely. Look for

opportunities to help others with no hidden agenda. It could be a small favor, like carrying groceries, or offering emotional support when a friend is down.

- **How to Do It:**
    - When you see someone struggling, ask if they would like help
    - Volunteer your time for tasks that do not bring you direct benefits, such as cleaning up a shared space at work
    - If you offer help, avoid expecting praise or payback
- **Why It Helps:**
    - Builds kindness and shows others you value them
    - Reminds you that the world does not revolve around your own needs

Use Self-Reflection Exercises

Taking time each day to reflect on your behavior helps you notice patterns you might miss otherwise. You could write in a notebook or use a simple mental check at the end of the day.

- **What to Reflect On:**
    - Times you felt the urge to talk only about yourself
    - Moments you showed support or empathy
    - Situations where you controlled or dismissed someone's feelings
- **Why It Helps:**
    - Raises awareness of triggers and improvements
    - Builds accountability for your actions

Allow Others to Lead

If you often like to be in control, practice stepping back. In a group project or outing, let someone else make a decision. Even if you feel their plan is not the same as yours, give it a fair chance.

- **How to Do It:**
    - Say, "I'm open to your ideas. What do you think we should do?"
    - Resist any urge to say your own plan is better
    - If doubts arise, calmly share them, but still respect the other person's lead

- Why It Helps:
  - Teaches you that you are not the only one with good ideas
  - Builds trust and respect among team members or friends

Limit Shifting Blame

Accepting responsibility is important. When something goes wrong, try to see your part in it before pointing fingers. Even if others played a role, be honest about your own errors.

- **Steps to Achieve This:**
  - When a situation fails, ask yourself, "What could I have done better?"
  - Apologize if you made a mistake
  - Focus on finding a solution rather than looking for someone to blame
- **Why It Helps:**
  - Encourages honesty and humility
  - Improves relationships by showing you can own up to mistakes

Stop Comparing Yourself to Others

For some people, self-centered habits come from always measuring themselves against others. They either try to prove they are better or feel insecure if they think they are not. Breaking free from the cycle of comparison helps you think less about yourself and more about the bigger picture.

- **How to Do It:**
  - Notice when you compare ("They have more than me" or "I'm smarter than them")
  - Remind yourself that everyone has different strengths and weaknesses
  - Shift focus toward your own growth, not how you rank against others
- **Why It Helps:**
  - Reduces envy or arrogance
  - Lets you see others as people to connect with, not as rivals

Ask for Honest Feedback

Sometimes, we do not see our own behavior clearly. Ask someone you trust—a friend, partner, or family member—to give you honest feedback about how you act. This can be scary, but it can also provide insights.

- **How to Do It:**
    - Explain you are trying to work on being less self-centered
    - Request a clear example of where you might have gone wrong
    - Listen without arguing or making excuses
- **Why It Helps:**
    - You learn about blind spots
    - It fosters closer relationships because you show humility

Recognize the Value of Others' Achievements

If you find yourself dismissing someone else's good news, pause and think about how they must feel. Offering genuine support or a kind word can help you shift from a self-focused mindset to one that values others.

- **Practical Ideas:**
    - Tell them, "That's really impressive," and ask how they feel about their accomplishment
    - Avoid downplaying their success or bringing up your own success right after
- **Why It Helps:**
    - Builds positive connections
    - Trains you to share in others' happiness

Try Small Acts of Kindness Daily

If you want to reduce self-focus, set a goal to do one small kind act each day. This does not have to be huge—something simple like holding the door for someone or complimenting a friend's effort.

- **Examples:**
    - Offering to make coffee for someone at work
    - Writing a note of thanks for a helpful coworker
    - Checking in on a friend who seems stressed
- **Why It Helps:**
    - Boosts a sense of community and caring
    - Reminds you that other people's well-being matters

Avoid Taking More Than You Give
If you notice that you ask for favors often, try to give back an equal amount or more. This might mean offering help before you even need something in return.

- **How to Do It:**
    - Keep track of how often you ask for help vs. how often you offer it
    - Make a conscious effort to give more than you receive
- **Why It Helps:**
    - Balances out relationships
    - Shows others that you value fairness

Set Personal Goals for Improvement
Reducing self-centered habits is a process that benefits from clear targets. Decide what behaviors you want to change and create a plan for each. For instance, if you struggle with interrupting, aim to let the other person finish their thought at least three times in every conversation.

- **Creating Good Goals:**
    - Be specific ("I will let others speak first in our team meeting")
    - Measure progress ("Today, I managed to wait until my friend finished talking each time")
- **Why It Helps:**
    - Gives you a clear direction
    - Helps you see improvement in small steps

Learn to Handle Criticism Calmly
One reason self-focused people get upset easily is that criticism feels like a threat. Practice listening to feedback without blowing up or breaking down. If the criticism is valid, thank the person and see how you might improve. If it is not, politely respond with your view.

- **How to Do It:**
    - Breathe deeply when you hear a critique
    - Say, "I understand what you're saying. Can you share an example?"
    - Decide if their feedback is fair. If yes, accept it. If no, calmly explain your thoughts
- **Why It Helps:**
    - Shows you are open-minded
    - Builds respect, even with people who disagree

Give Genuine Compliments

One way to shift attention off yourself is to notice good things about others. Offering a thoughtful compliment can help you learn to value the people around you. Be specific, kind, and honest when you compliment.

- **Examples:**
    - "You spoke very clearly during that presentation. It kept everyone interested."
    - "Your idea really solved our problem. Great job."
- **Why It Helps:**
    - Encourages you to see the positive qualities in others
    - Helps them feel seen and appreciated

Balance Alone Time and Group Activities

Sometimes, self-focused habits grow because we do not spend enough time with others. If you spend most of your days alone, it is easy to forget other people's feelings and needs. Try to keep a balanced schedule that includes interactions with friends, family, or group events.

- **How to Do It:**
    - Plan regular meetups or calls with friends
    - Join a club or team if you feel you need practice cooperating
- **Why It Helps:**
    - In a group, you have to consider different points of view
    - Repeated contact with others can soften self-centered patterns

Develop Fair Expectations

If you tend to expect special treatment, work on adjusting your mindset. For instance, at a restaurant, do not demand the best seat just because you think you deserve it. Treat staff and strangers with basic kindness, the same way you would want to be treated if the roles were reversed.

- **How to Do It:**
    - Wait your turn in lines or discussions
    - Accept that you are not always first
    - Remember that each person also has their own wants and feelings
- **Why It Helps:**
    - Teaches you not to see yourself as the center of every situation

- Encourages a more respectful approach toward people you do not know well

Seek Healthy Outlets for Emotions

Some self-centered habits come from strong emotions you might not know how to handle. If you find yourself lashing out or seeking attention when upset, try healthier ways to manage feelings. This could include writing about how you feel, talking to a trusted friend, or doing a calming activity.

- **Ideas for Healthy Outlets:**
    - Go for a walk or do light exercise
    - Listen to music that soothes you
    - Write in a personal notebook to process frustration
- **Why It Helps:**
    - Prevents you from taking out your emotions on others
    - Teaches you that seeking attention is not the only way to cope

It is important to acknowledge your steps toward improvement, but do so in a manner that does not bring all attention back to you. Perhaps you make a note in your journal about a conversation that went well because you listened more. Or you share with a close friend that you are proud you did not interrupt anyone today. Do it calmly, and remind yourself that growth is about long-term changes, not praise.

- **How to Do It:**
    - Reflect in private on what you have done better
    - Give yourself silent credit for trying
    - If sharing with someone, make it a small statement ("I'm happy I was able to listen better today")
- **Why It Helps:**
    - Reinforces positive changes
    - Keeps you grounded and avoids slipping back into bragging

---

Staying Motivated and Moving Forward

Cutting down on self-centered habits can be challenging at first. You may slip up from time to time. It is part of learning. The key is to be consistent and honest with yourself about your progress.

- **Set Reasonable Goals:** Do not try to change every habit at once. Pick one or two key behaviors and focus on improving those first.
- **Seek Support:** Ask a friend or family member to remind you if they see old patterns. This is not to shame you, but to help you notice when you might not see it yourself.
- **Reward Yourself Thoughtfully:** Recognize your efforts in ways that do not feed self-importance. For example, treat yourself to a quiet evening of reading or doing something calming once you make real improvements.
- **Stay Open to Feedback:** Even as you improve, keep asking for input. It can reveal new areas to work on.

As you reduce self-centered habits, you will likely see changes in how people respond to you. They may open up more, show appreciation, and trust you with their own thoughts and feelings. You may also notice less inner stress, since you are no longer always worried about your image or needing constant attention. Over time, these healthier behaviors can lead to a deeper sense of calm and a richer connection with the people in your life.

In the next chapters, we will look at different ways to grow and maintain empathy, along with methods to find calm within yourself. But for now, focus on one or two of the steps listed here. With patience and honesty, you will find that small changes can build into lasting improvements.

Chapter 5: Learning About Empathy

Empathy is the ability to understand how someone else feels. It involves seeing a situation through another person's eyes, rather than just your own. When you have empathy, you do more than notice that someone looks sad or upset—you try to feel what they feel on the inside. This chapter explains why empathy is so important, how it differs from related ideas like sympathy, and why growing empathy can help move away from harmful self-focus.

Understanding Empathy vs. Sympathy
Many people confuse empathy with sympathy. Sympathy is when you feel sorry for someone's situation. Empathy goes deeper, because you not only feel sorry, but you also try to imagine that you are in their shoes.

- **Sympathy Example:** You might say, "I'm sorry you're having a bad day," but not truly think about what your friend is going through.
- **Empathy Example:** You might say, "I'm sorry you're having a bad day," and then think about how you would feel if you were in their place. You might follow up by asking, "Is there anything I can do to help?"

Empathy leads you to act with kindness, while sympathy might just keep you at a distance.

Why Empathy Matters
When people practice empathy, they can form closer bonds with friends, family, and coworkers. It helps create an atmosphere of care and respect because everyone feels understood. Empathy can also reduce arguments and help resolve conflicts more peacefully.

- **Improved Relationships:** People who feel understood are more likely to trust you. They tend to open up, which allows deeper connections.
- **Less Conflict:** Empathy helps you see where the other person is coming from, which can calm tense situations.

- **Personal Growth:** Trying to see from another's perspective makes you more open-minded. You start to grasp that other people have their own stories and feelings that matter.

How Empathy Relates to Narcissism

Individuals who struggle with narcissistic traits often focus on themselves and overlook how others feel. Empathy is the opposite of that approach. Learning to see beyond your own thoughts can lower self-centered habits. Instead of always thinking, "How does this affect me?" you start to ask, "How does this affect the other person?"

- **Shifting Focus:** Empathy puts attention on someone else's needs, not your own.
- **Building Compassion:** With empathy, you care about what others are experiencing, which can stop you from hurting them with careless words or actions.

Emotional Empathy and Cognitive Empathy

There are two main parts of empathy: emotional empathy and cognitive empathy.

- **Emotional Empathy:** You pick up on the other person's feelings and might even feel a bit of their emotion. For instance, if a friend is crying, you sense their sadness and feel a bit sad yourself.
- **Cognitive Empathy:** You understand what the other person might be thinking, even if you do not share the same emotion. For example, you see someone who lost a big game, and you think, "They are probably disappointed and worried about letting their team down," without necessarily feeling upset yourself.

Both emotional and cognitive empathy are useful. Emotional empathy helps you connect on a heartfelt level, while cognitive empathy helps you offer solutions or support in a thoughtful way.

Common Barriers to Empathy

Some people want to be more caring but struggle to do so. Here are a few reasons empathy might be blocked:

- **Self-Centered Thought Patterns:** When you are mostly thinking about yourself, it is hard to notice what others are going through.

- **Lack of Exposure to Different People:** If you only spend time with people who are just like you, it can be harder to see life from other viewpoints.
- **Fear of Emotional Pain:** Empathy sometimes means sharing in someone else's sadness. This can feel overwhelming, so some avoid it to protect themselves.
- **Past Hurt:** If you were hurt or felt unimportant in the past, you might shut yourself off and focus only on your own needs.

Signs That You Need More Empathy

You might guess that you need more empathy if you notice these behaviors:

- You are often unaware when someone close to you is upset.
- Friends and family say you do not really "get" them.
- You find yourself thinking other people's problems are not your concern.
- You sometimes use harsh words and then feel surprised when people are hurt.

These signs do not mean you are hopeless. They are simply clues that you can work on strengthening your ability to understand others.

The Positive Effects of Growing Empathy

Working on empathy can lead to many good changes in your life:

- **Better Communication:** When you try to see others' feelings, you also learn to speak more kindly.
- **Deeper Friendships:** Empathy makes it easier to support friends. They, in turn, feel safe to come to you with their joys and troubles.
- **Reduced Anxiety in Social Settings:** Being empathetic can help you handle disagreements and misunderstandings with a calm mindset.
- **More Happiness:** Caring about others often brings a sense of fulfillment.

Simple Thoughts That Encourage Empathy

Sometimes, empathy starts with a shift in thinking. Instead of focusing on your own plan or feelings, try one of these thoughts:

- "I wonder what their day has been like."

- "How would I feel if that happened to me?"
- "Maybe there is more to their actions than I realize."

These quick questions can remind you that everyone has a unique story.

Why Empathy Is More Than Just Being Nice
Being polite or friendly is not the same as truly showing empathy. Politeness can be surface-level: smiling, greeting someone, and using good manners. Empathy goes deeper because it tries to connect with the real feelings underneath. A person can be polite without caring at all about how you feel, but empathy aims to understand those feelings and respond in a caring way.

Empathy in Different Settings

- **Home:** With family members, empathy helps each person feel valued. Parents who show empathy teach children that their emotions are heard. Siblings who show empathy get along better.
- **Work or School:** Empathy helps when conflicts arise in a group project or team effort. Understanding each member's struggles can lead to fair solutions.
- **Friendships:** Friends who are empathetic will be there for each other through good times and bad times.
- **Romantic Relationships:** Empathy helps couples handle disagreements without causing deep emotional harm.

The Role of Emotion in Empathy
Emotions play a big role. When you see a close friend cry, your own heart might feel heavy. This shared emotion motivates you to act, like giving them a hug or offering comforting words. Some people find it tough to manage these feelings, but with practice, they learn to channel them in ways that help both themselves and the other person.

Empathy and Self-Awareness
You cannot show empathy if you do not have some awareness of your own emotions. If you are shut off from your own feelings, you may also be shut off from understanding others. Learning to identify your emotions—happy, sad, worried, angry—builds a stronger base for recognizing emotions in other people as well.

Overcoming the Fear of Vulnerability

Showing empathy can make people feel exposed. If you say, "I know you're hurting, and I really feel for you," you open your heart. Some worry that this might make them look weak. In reality, healthy vulnerability often brings people closer. It shows sincerity and tells the other person, "You're not alone in this."

Myths About Empathy

- **Myth 1: Empathy is only for sensitive people.** In truth, anyone can learn to be empathetic, no matter their personality.
- **Myth 2: Empathy means you must fix everyone's problems.** Showing empathy does not mean you must solve everything. Sometimes, just listening and understanding is enough.
- **Myth 3: Empathy makes you soft.** Empathy does not erase firmness or clarity. You can be empathetic and still hold someone accountable if they are in the wrong.

Emotional Intelligence

Empathy is part of emotional intelligence, which also includes skills like managing your own feelings, motivating yourself, and handling relationships in a healthy way. A person with high emotional intelligence is likely to be good at caring for others and showing kindness.

How Empathy Grows Over Time

Empathy is not something that appears instantly if you have never worked on it. It grows little by little:

- **Listening to People's Stories**: The more you listen, the more you understand the variety of feelings people have.
- **Reading**: Some stories or articles put you into the minds of characters or real individuals, letting you see life through their eyes.
- **Practice in Small Interactions**: Even small talks with neighbors or classmates can help. Ask how they are and pay attention to their answers.
- **Reflect on Conversations**: Think about how you responded. Did you offer comfort or understanding? If not, how could you do better next time?

Empathy and Cultural Differences

Different cultures have various ways of expressing emotions. In one culture, hugging might be a common sign of support. In another, a simple nod or pat on the back might be preferred. Being empathetic means learning how people from different backgrounds show or hide their feelings. This sensitivity helps avoid misunderstandings and fosters mutual respect.

Balancing Empathy with Self-Care

Some worry that if they care too much about others, they will be overwhelmed. It is true that constantly taking on other people's hurts can weigh you down if you do not also look after yourself. Empathy does not mean you ignore your own health or happiness. It means you show kindness and understanding while also acknowledging your own limits.

Empathy in Group Situations

When you are in a group—like a club, a class, or a work team—empathy can help create an environment where everyone feels secure. For example, if one team member is shy and rarely speaks, an empathetic teammate might notice that shyness and actively invite them to share. This can bring out ideas that might otherwise remain hidden.

True Stories of Empathy

- **Friendship Example:** A teenager who saw their classmate crying after a failed test asked them to sit together at lunch. They listened, offered a few kind words, and made the person feel less alone.
- **Family Example:** An older sibling noticed their younger brother feeling left out. They decided to include him in a board game, explaining the rules carefully and praising him for trying. This display of empathy boosted the younger brother's confidence.
- **Work Example:** A manager with empathy recognized an employee was stressed. They adjusted the workload and offered a quick check-in each morning, leading to better morale and performance.

Practical Strategies to Start Building Empathy

- **Ask Questions:** Instead of assuming you know how someone feels, ask, "How are you handling this?" or "What's going on in your mind?"
- **Look for Nonverbal Cues:** Notice body language, tone of voice, and facial expressions. If someone is hunched over or speaking softly, they might be sad or anxious.
- **Wait Before Judging:** If a friend acts grumpy, pause and consider other reasons. Maybe they are tired or have a problem at home. Jumping to conclusions can stop empathy in its tracks.

- **Match Your Response to Their Emotion:** If someone is overjoyed, share in that excitement. If they are scared, speak softly or offer reassurance.

Empathy's Role in Personal Peace

Caring about other people's feelings can also help you find calm. When you understand someone else's perspective, you often see that conflicts might not be as big as they seemed. Empathy can lower frustration and anger, providing a sense of calm in your own heart.

Common Mistakes When Trying to Be Empathetic

- **Making It About You:** Even when trying to connect, you might accidentally steer the conversation back to your own experiences. Instead, keep the focus on them.
- **Offering Quick Fixes:** Sometimes, a person mainly wants to be heard. Jumping straight to "Here's what you should do" can block true empathy.
- **Pretending to Understand:** If you have never felt what they feel, be honest. It is okay to say, "I can't fully imagine how hard this is, but I want to support you."

Empathy as a Key Step Away from Narcissism

If you have noticed self-centered traits in your life, increasing empathy is one of the strongest ways to shift your perspective. Each time you stop to think about another's feelings, you weaken the habit of focusing only on yourself. Over time, this can significantly change how you relate to others.

Summing Up the Power of Empathy

Empathy transforms how we treat one another. It breaks down barriers and lets us see each other as complete people with feelings, hopes, and worries. For someone who has struggled with narcissistic traits, learning empathy can feel like stepping into a new world, one that has more warmth and genuine connection.

This chapter has covered why empathy matters, how it can be blocked, the many benefits it brings, and some initial methods to begin growing it. The next chapter will build on these ideas, showing more hands-on ways to practice empathy every day. By adding action to these insights, you can move closer to healthy relationships and a more balanced sense of self.

Chapter 6: Helpful Methods to Show Empathy

Building on the idea of empathy from the previous chapter, this chapter focuses on practical methods you can use to show empathy in everyday life. By learning specific actions, you can turn the concept of empathy into something real and helpful. You will find that these methods do not require special resources or lots of training. All you need is a willingness to step outside your own head and care about how another person feels.

Active Listening
One of the most direct ways to show empathy is to listen attentively. This is called "active listening," because it involves more than just hearing words. It is about giving your full attention and responding in a way that shows you truly want to understand.

- **Steps to Active Listening:**
    - Put aside distractions like phones or laptops.
    - Maintain eye contact without staring.
    - Nod or give small cues to let them know you hear them.
    - Summarize what they said: "So you feel upset because your teammate didn't help?"
    - Ask gentle questions: "What do you think would help right now?"

This approach tells the other person that you are present in the moment and not merely waiting for your turn to talk.

Validating Feelings
To validate someone's feelings is to recognize them as real and important. Instead of brushing off their emotions, you reflect them back.

- **Examples of Validation Phrases:**
    - "I see why that would be frustrating."
    - "I can understand how that might feel scary."
    - "It makes sense that you're sad."

These small statements show that you are not questioning their right to feel a certain way. You are acknowledging it.

Open-Ended Questions
Asking open-ended questions allows the other person to share more about their thoughts and emotions. Unlike yes/no questions, open-ended ones encourage deeper conversation.

- **Examples:**
  - "How did that situation affect you?"
  - "What worries you the most about this?"
  - "Can you tell me more about what happened?"

Open-ended questions signal that you are truly interested in understanding them, rather than seeking quick answers.

Reflective Responses
After someone shares, try reflecting what they have said in your own words. This helps them feel heard and also confirms you got their point.

- **Reflective Response Template:**
  - "So what I hear you saying is…"
  - "It sounds like you were disappointed when…"
  - "You seem upset because…"

Reflecting not only shows you are listening, but also gives the person a chance to correct any misunderstanding.

Nonverbal Empathy
People often speak through body language. Showing empathy can be done with a comforting touch on the shoulder (if appropriate), a soft smile, or a concerned look that matches the speaker's mood. Some people find physical contact comforting, but always be mindful of personal space and what the other person prefers.

Give Others the Spotlight
In many conversations, we rush to talk about our own experiences. To show empathy, hold back on that urge and let the other person keep the focus on themselves.

- **Practical Tip:**
    - Each time you feel the need to jump in with your own story, take a mental step back. Ask another question about their situation instead.

This method helps break the habit of placing yourself at the center of every talk.

Encouraging Words
Empathy can also be about encouraging someone. For example, if a friend is upset about failing a test, you can say, "I know you are feeling down, and I would too if I were in your place. But I believe you can do better next time with a little help."

- **Why It Works:**
    - Shows understanding of their feelings
    - Offers hope without dismissing their current struggle

Offer Help Without Pushing
Sometimes, empathy means offering help or support in a non-pushy way. Let them know you are willing to assist, but also respect their boundaries. For instance, you can say, "Is there anything I can do right now to lighten the load?" rather than "You need to do this or that."

Practice Empathy in Small Moments
Empathy is not limited to big, serious problems. You can show empathy in everyday life:

- **At the Grocery Store:** If you see someone looking confused in the aisle, you might ask if they need help finding something.
- **With Strangers:** If someone bumps into you and looks stressed, a calm "Are you okay?" can help them feel less embarrassed.
- **During Group Activities:** Notice who is quiet and invite them to share.

Adjusting to Different Personalities
Some people talk easily about their feelings, while others do not. Showing empathy means adjusting to their style. If the person is reserved, give them more space and time. Maybe they prefer writing down their thoughts or talking one-on-one instead of in a group.

Cultural Awareness

Be aware that gestures of empathy can differ across cultures. What is comforting in one culture might be awkward in another. If you are unsure, you can quietly check in by saying, "Would you be okay with a hug?" or "I don't want to intrude. Is it alright if I stay with you for a while?"

Listening to Tone and Words

Pay attention to how someone speaks, not just what they say. If their voice trembles, they might be holding back tears. If they speak quickly, maybe they are anxious. Matching your response to their tone shows you are picking up on clues.

When Empathy Feels Uncomfortable

Sometimes, hearing about someone's pain can be tough. You might feel unsure of what to say or worry that you will make things worse. In such moments, it is okay to admit, "I'm not totally sure how to help, but I want you to know I care." Even that honesty can be a form of empathy, because it shows you are trying to be real.

Empathy in Conflict Situations

When arguments happen, showing empathy for the other person's viewpoint can calm things down. It does not mean you agree with them completely, but that you are trying to see how they reached their perspective.

- **Method:**
    - Let them express their side fully before responding.
    - Repeat what they said in your own words, so they know you heard them.
    - Then explain your side without personal attacks.

This approach can prevent a fight from becoming nasty. Both people feel respected, which often leads to finding middle ground.

Use "I" Statements

In conflicts or tough conversations, "I" statements can keep empathy going. Instead of saying, "You never listen," try, "I feel unheard when I share my ideas, because it seems like you change the subject quickly." This approach takes blame off the other person and focuses on your own feelings.

Story Sharing

While you should not make every conversation about yourself, sometimes it can help to share a brief story if it directly relates to what the other person is feeling. This kind of sharing can show you truly understand their emotions.

- **How to Do It Correctly:**
    - Keep it short. The main goal is to connect, not shift focus permanently to you.
    - End by bringing the conversation back to them: "That was my experience. How does that compare to yours?"

Helping Children Learn Empathy

If you have younger siblings, children, or spend time with kids, you can show them empathy by letting them express their feelings freely and guiding them on how to handle those emotions.

- **Example:** If a child is upset because a friend took their toy, encourage them to use words like, "I feel sad because I want to play with it." Then, help them see the friend's view: "Your friend might also like that toy. Maybe you two can take turns."

This early teaching helps kids grow up thinking about others.

Apologizing with Empathy

When you have caused hurt, a genuine apology includes an empathetic understanding of how the other person feels. For example, you might say, "I realize my words were harsh, and they caused you distress. I understand why you are upset, and I want you to know I'm truly sorry. I'll do better."

- **Why It Matters:**
    - It shows you do not just regret the action; you also care about the impact.

Encourage Others to Speak for Themselves

Empathy sometimes means you do not speak on someone else's behalf unless they ask you to. Instead, invite them to share their feelings or needs directly. This shows respect for their voice.

Building Empathy Through Reading or Media

Watching films or reading books can help you practice empathy. By immersing yourself in a character's life, you practice seeing the world from a new perspective. Then, you can apply that skill in real conversations.

Mindfulness Exercises

Practicing mindfulness—staying fully in the present—can sharpen your awareness of others. If you find your thoughts wandering when someone speaks, bring yourself back to the moment by focusing on their words or their expressions.

Check In Later

Empathy does not have to end when the conversation ends. If someone told you about a problem, reach out a day or two later to see how they are doing. This follow-up shows that you genuinely care, not just in the moment but afterward too.

Keep Your Ego in Check

Even when you are trying to be empathetic, pride can sneak in. You might start thinking, "I'm such a great person for helping!" If you notice this, gently remind yourself that empathy is about the other person. The goal is to reduce the self-centered outlook, not polish your own image.

Role-Playing for Practice

If you are unsure how to show empathy in certain situations, it can help to role-play with a trusted friend or family member. Pretend one of you is going through a tough time, and the other listens with empathy. Then switch roles. This exercise can prepare you for real-life moments.

Accepting People's Chosen Boundaries

Sometimes, people may not be ready to share more or receive comfort. Empathy respects this and does not force closeness. You can say, "I'm here if you ever want to talk," and then give them space.

Using Technology Thoughtfully

Modern life often involves texting, email, or social media. You can still show empathy there:

- **Texting:** Send a genuine message asking how they feel, rather than just saying "Sorry."

- **Social Media:** If someone posts about a tough day, offer a supportive comment. But if the topic is private, maybe send a private message instead of a public reply.

Always keep in mind that online communication can be misunderstood, so be gentle and clear.

A Word About Empathy Fatigue
If you constantly care for others without any pause, you might face empathy fatigue. This can make you feel exhausted or numb. To avoid this, remember to take breaks, talk to someone you trust about your own feelings, and do things that help you relax.

Signs You Are Growing in Empathy

- People tell you they feel comfortable opening up to you.
- You handle disagreements with less anger.
- You notice how others feel, even if they do not directly tell you.
- You feel more connected to friends and family.

Overcoming Self-Focus with Daily Empathy
The daily act of thinking about someone else's point of view can chip away at old, self-focused habits. Each time you choose to ask how a coworker is feeling instead of talking about your own day, you build a new pattern in your mind—one that leans toward caring rather than self-interest.

Final Thoughts on Empathy in Action
Showing empathy is not about being perfect. You might still have moments where you slip into old behaviors or fail to see someone's feelings right away. The point is to keep trying. Every time you pause to listen, ask questions, and respond with kindness, you strengthen an important life skill.

Empathy is one of the strongest tools in stepping away from harmful self-focus. It can lead to stronger friendships, better family bonds, and a sense of calm within yourself. By practicing the methods in this chapter—active listening, validating feelings, offering help, and so on—you can make empathy a natural part of who you are. It will become something you do without even thinking about it, bringing more warmth to your life and to the lives of those around you.

Chapter 7: Steps for Inner Peace

Feeling calm on the inside can make your entire life better. Inner peace is a sense of stillness and comfort in your heart and mind. It is not about ignoring problems; it is about finding a steady state that helps you handle whatever comes your way. If you have struggled with self-focused habits, it might feel difficult at first to slow down and find calm. Still, there are ways to bring a softer and more balanced mood into daily life. This chapter will show you practical steps you can try each day to move toward a calmer state of being.

Start Your Day Slowly
Many people wake up and jump right into tasks or worries. This rush can make your mind busy before you have even had breakfast. Instead, try taking a few minutes in the morning to sit quietly, sip a warm drink, or look out a window. Pay attention to how your body feels. Notice if you are stiff, tired, or rested. Breathe gently for a moment. This practice sets a peaceful tone.

a. **Simple Morning Activity:**
- Sit up in bed or on a chair.
- Breathe in gently through your nose for a count of three, then breathe out through your mouth for a count of three.
- Repeat this five or six times, keeping your focus on the breath.

This small step can help you face the day with a calm mind. Even if you have a busy schedule, a short pause in the morning can remind you that peace is possible.

Create a Soothing Space
It helps to have a spot, no matter how small, that feels safe and relaxing. It might be a corner of your room with a soft cushion or a comfy chair. You could keep a blanket, a lamp with gentle light, or a few items that bring you a sense of calm—like a simple rock, a small plant, or a smooth piece of wood you found on a walk.

    b. **Why This Helps:**
        - Having a spot to go to when you feel unsettled can quickly ease stress.
        - Your mind starts to connect that spot with feeling calmer.

Give Your Thoughts Some Room
Our minds can race with worries, plans, or regrets. Inner peace means letting those thoughts come and go without pushing them away or clinging to them. When a troubling thought appears, notice it: "Okay, I'm feeling worried about work." Then, let it pass. Picture it like a cloud that floats across the sky.

    c. **Practical Tip:**
        - If a thought keeps repeating, write it down on a piece of paper. This can help clear your head. After writing, take a slow breath and remind yourself that the thought is now noted.

Practice Self-Acceptance
A key part of inner peace is learning to accept yourself as you are in this moment. That means noticing your feelings—even the ones you do not like—without judging them. You can still aim to make better choices, but start with seeing your current thoughts and emotions clearly. If you try to pretend they do not exist, you may end up feeling worse in the long run.

    d. **How to Accept Yourself:**
        - When you feel upset, pause and name it: "I feel tense right now."
        - Take a deep breath and say, "It is okay for me to feel this way. I can handle it."

Accepting your emotions can help them calm down sooner. You are not letting them control you. You are simply giving them space.

Slow, Steady Breathing
Deep breathing might sound simple, but it is a powerful way to lower stress and create calm. When you breathe slowly, you send signals to your body that you are safe. This can help reduce the rush of nervous energy.

    e. **Exercise:**
        - Sit upright and close your eyes if you feel comfortable.

- Breathe in through your nose for a count of four. Hold for a brief moment.
- Breathe out through your mouth for a count of four.
- Repeat for a few minutes, focusing only on the breath.

Even a brief session of slow breathing can make you feel more at ease, especially if you do it regularly.

Gentle Movement

Movement does not have to be intense. Simple activities, like walking or gentle stretching, can relax your body and clear your mind. When you walk, pay attention to each step, how your foot touches the ground, and the sounds around you. This form of mindful movement can help release tension.

f. **Example of Gentle Movement Routine:**
   - Walk at a calm pace for 10 minutes. Notice the breeze or the warmth of the sun.
   - Stop and stretch your arms overhead. Breathe in as you stretch up, breathe out as you lower your arms.
   - Continue walking, staying aware of how your body feels.

Short Breaks During the Day

Modern life can be packed with tasks and messages. Setting aside small breaks can help keep your mind from feeling overloaded. During these breaks, pause and do something calming, such as:

g. Listening to soft music
h. Taking a few deep breaths at your desk
i. Looking at a nature photo or a calming color

These pauses act like mini-resets for your mind. You could schedule them on your phone or watch so you do not forget.

Kind Self-Talk

A lot of mental stress comes from harsh thoughts we aim at ourselves. If you slip up or make a mistake, how do you speak to yourself in your mind? Replacing mean or critical statements with kinder ones will help you feel less tense.

j. **Examples:**

- Harsh Thought: "I can't believe I messed up again. I'm so useless."
- Kind Thought: "Everyone makes mistakes. I'll try to fix it and do better next time."

Small changes in the words you use can have a big effect on how calm you feel.

Choose Simple Pleasures

Inner peace grows when you find small, peaceful moments in daily life. Rather than chasing big excitement or constant praise, look for simple joys. It might be the feel of warm water on your hands when you wash dishes or the soft sound of the wind outside your window.

k. **Ideas for Simple Pleasures:**
   - Savor the taste of your food instead of rushing.
   - Spend a minute admiring the sky or a tree.
   - Light a gentle-smelling candle while reading.

Limit Information Overload

Constant news updates, social media scrolling, or screens can keep your mind in a busy state. If you find yourself feeling anxious or restless, consider limiting how often you check your phone or other devices.

- **Practical Step:**
  - Set a rule for yourself: "I will put my phone aside for the first hour of the day."
  - If you worry about missing something, give a close friend or family member a different way to reach you in an emergency.

Focus on What You Can Control

Worrying about things outside your power can rob you of peace. Instead, ask, "Is this something I can do something about right now?" If the answer is yes, take a small, clear step. If the answer is no, try to accept that fact and direct your attention elsewhere.

- **Example:**
  - If you are fretting about tomorrow's weather, remind yourself you cannot change it. Plan to take an umbrella if rain is likely, then move on.

Learn to Let Go of Grudges
Holding onto anger or resentment can eat away at your peace. Letting go does not mean what happened was fine; it means you choose not to let that anger control you. You can do this by writing a short note about the issue, stating your feelings, then throwing the note away. This act can be symbolic, signaling that you are setting down the emotional weight.

Relaxing Your Body
Sometimes we hold tension in our bodies without noticing—tight shoulders, clenched fists, or a stiff neck. A relaxation exercise can ease these tight spots.

- **Body Scan Exercise:**
    1. Close your eyes and take a slow breath.
    2. Start at your feet. Notice any tightness there. Try to relax that area.
    3. Move up to your calves, thighs, stomach, chest, shoulders, arms, and face.
    4. Spend a few seconds on each part, releasing the tension with each exhale.

By the time you reach your head, you may feel softer and more at peace.

Say "No" When Needed
If you tend to say "yes" to every request, you might end up overwhelmed, leaving no time to rest. Learning to say "no" politely can protect your peace. You do not have to explain yourself too much. A simple, "I'm sorry, but I can't do that right now," is enough.

- **Why This Matters:**
    - Saying "no" helps you keep a balanced schedule.
    - It also sends a message to yourself that your time and well-being matter.

Write It Out
Journaling, or writing down thoughts, can be a helpful tool for inner peace. You can keep a small notebook by your bed or in a desk drawer. When you feel uneasy, write about what is on your mind. The act of placing words on paper can untangle knots of worry or sadness.

- **Simple Journal Prompt:**

- "Today I feel _____ because _____."
- "One thing I can do to be calmer right now is _____."

Spend Time in Nature
Nature has a calming effect on many people. It might be a local park, a backyard garden, or even a single tree outside your home. Take a moment to watch leaves move in the breeze or to listen to birds. These small details can ground you in the present moment.

- **How to Include This in Daily Life:**
    - Walk outside during a break.
    - Sit on a bench or porch for a few minutes after work.
    - If you cannot go outdoors, look at pictures of forests, mountains, or oceans.

Practice Gratitude
When your mind is focused on what is missing or wrong, you can feel stressed. Shifting your focus to things you are thankful for can bring calm and contentment. This does not have to be dramatic. Even small things, like a tasty meal or a gentle breeze, can make you feel a bit brighter.

- **Quick Activity:**
    - Each night, think of three things that went well or that you appreciated.
    - Write them in a small notebook or on your phone.

Healthy Habits
Your physical well-being and your mental state connect closely. Simple habits like getting enough sleep, eating balanced meals, and drinking water can boost your mood and sense of calm. If you stay up too late or skip meals, you may feel cranky or anxious, making it harder to feel at peace.

Speak Kindly to Others
Speaking kindly to friends, family, or even strangers can calm your own mind. Words carry emotion, and when you choose gentler ones, you create a calmer atmosphere. Pay attention to your tone and volume, too. Even if you have to disagree, do it without shouting or belittling.

Notice Moments of Calm
You might experience small moments when you feel truly at ease—a few seconds

of silence before bedtime, a peaceful drive with no traffic, or a quiet afternoon reading a book. Pay attention to these moments. By noticing them, you train your mind to recognize peace more often.

- **Tip:**
    - When you find such a moment, gently tell yourself, "This is calm. I appreciate this."
    - Let that feeling sink in for a few breaths.

Encourage Yourself Through Setbacks

Finding inner peace does not mean you will never feel stressed or upset. You will still face problems. The difference is in how you respond. When a setback happens—maybe an argument with a friend or a bad grade—be patient with yourself. Acknowledge what happened and decide on a calm, constructive action.

- **Example:**
    - If you failed an exam, allow yourself to feel upset for a short time. Then, plan new study methods or ask someone for help. By focusing on the next helpful step, you protect your calm instead of staying in panic.

Take Time for Fun

Fun activities are not just for children. Grown-ups also need play. Doing something you truly enjoy—like a puzzle, a hobby, or a sport—can relax the mind and reduce stress. This is different from simply wasting time online. Aim for hobbies that bring you a sense of delight or let your mind rest from usual worries.

Let Go of Perfection

Chasing perfection is a sure way to stir up constant stress. You might worry that your project, your cooking, or your appearance is never good enough. Real peace comes from doing your best while accepting that nothing is ever flawless. If you always demand perfection, you set yourself up for endless frustration.

Build on Small Successes

If you manage to stay calm in a situation that used to make you panic, that is a real win. Maybe you spoke kindly during a tense meeting, or you paused to breathe when you felt your heart racing. Recognize these moments as proof that you can find more peace with practice. You do not need to make a big show of it or draw attention to yourself—simply note it in your mind.

Share Calm with Others
Peace can spread from one person to another. When you act calm and speak gently, it encourages others to do the same. If you notice a friend is upset, you can sit with them quietly or offer a gentle word. This not only helps them but also strengthens your own sense of calm, knowing you can be a peaceful presence.

Seek Help When Necessary
Sometimes, no matter how many calming steps you try, the stress or worry does not fade. In that case, it might help to speak with a professional, such as a counselor or therapist. Talking things out with someone trained to help can bring relief and open new paths toward peace.

Keep a Light Heart About Mistakes
Everyone slips or makes errors. Holding onto guilt can disturb your sense of calm. Instead of staying stuck in shame, recognize the mistake, fix what you can, and move on. This mindset respects the reality that humans are imperfect but can keep growing.

End Your Day with Calm
How you finish your day can affect how you sleep and how you feel the next morning. Try a simple evening routine: turn off bright screens at least 30 minutes before bed, do a short bit of stretching or breathing, and think of one nice thing that happened that day. Let your mind rest instead of dwelling on unfinished tasks.

Accept That Peace Takes Steady Practice
Do not expect to feel calm every hour of every day. Finding peace is an ongoing process that you work on steadily. Some days, you may feel relaxed; other days, you might feel all over the place. This does not mean you have failed. Each time you practice, you build a bit more ease into your life.

Summary
Inner peace is not about a perfect life or the absence of problems. It is about learning how to handle yourself in a calmer way, even in the face of stress or conflict. Small actions—like gentle breathing, short pauses, kind self-talk, and letting go of grudges—can add up to a lighter, softer approach to life. By starting with just one or two steps, you can begin to feel a greater sense of calm.

Chapter 8: Dealing with Anger and Pressure

Anger and pressure are common feelings that can arise from day-to-day problems, personal conflicts, or even from memories of past hurts. If these feelings are left unchecked, they can grow and harm your well-being and relationships. In this chapter, we will discuss how to spot early signs of anger or intense pressure and how to respond to them in a way that preserves your calm. By learning these methods, you can lower the risk of lashing out, blaming others, or falling back into harmful self-focused habits.

Why Anger and Pressure Matter
Anger is a strong feeling that can come from frustration, fear, or disappointment. Pressure can feel like a heavy weight on your shoulders—maybe from deadlines, life events, or people's expectations. When these emotions grow too large, they can lead to actions or words you regret. They can also push you away from empathy and thoughtfulness, because you are focused on escaping the discomfort in any way you can.

Understanding Early Signs
Recognizing anger or pressure in its early stages is key. You might notice:

- **Body Signals:** Tight chest, clenched jaw, sweating, or racing heart.
- **Thought Patterns:** "This isn't fair," "I'm going to lose it," or "I can't handle this."
- **Mood Shifts:** Feeling easily annoyed or wanting to snap at people for small issues.

By catching these signs early, you have a chance to calm down before the emotion takes over.

Pause and Take a Breath
When you notice anger or pressure rising, your first step can be a simple pause. Stop whatever you are doing—if possible—and take a slow breath. This gives you a few seconds to break the cycle of heated thoughts.

- **Quick Breathing Trick:**
    1. Inhale through your nose for a count of three.

2. Hold your breath for one second.
3. Exhale gently through your mouth for a count of three.

Doing this a few times can lower the intensity of your anger or tension.

Name the Feeling
Sometimes anger can mask other emotions like sadness, fear, or shame. By naming what you really feel, you make it more manageable. Saying, "I feel scared" or "I feel unfairly treated" can shift your focus from raw anger to the actual cause of your distress.

- **Why It Works:**
    1. It makes the problem clearer, which helps you decide on a better action.
    2. It helps you communicate more honestly if you need to talk to someone about it.

Give Yourself Space
If you are in a heated discussion, it might help to step away for a bit. You can say, "I need a moment to cool down. Let's talk again in a few minutes." This break can prevent angry words that cause damage. Just be sure to come back when you have calmed down, so the issue is not ignored forever.

Replace Unhelpful Thoughts
Anger often comes with unhelpful thoughts like "They're doing this on purpose!" or "No one ever listens to me!" These thoughts may not reflect the full truth. Try to replace them with something more balanced:

- **Replacement Example:**
    1. Original Thought: "He never respects my time."
    2. New Thought: "He might have his own problems causing this delay. I will speak calmly to him about it."

Adjusting your thoughts can lower the flames of anger and bring a more logical approach.

Healthy Expression of Anger
Bottling up anger can lead to an outburst later. Expressing it in a respectful way is far better. This might mean:

- Writing a letter (that you may not even send) detailing how you feel
- Talking to a close friend or a professional counselor about your frustration
- Using "I" statements in a calm conversation with the person who upset you (for example, "I feel upset because I thought we had an agreement, and it was broken")

The key is to let the emotion out without harming yourself or others.

Release Tension with Physical Actions
Anger and pressure can build up energy in your body. Safe physical actions can release that energy:

- **Options:**
    1. Take a brisk walk or jog
    2. Punch a pillow (in a safe, private place)
    3. Do simple exercises like push-ups or jumping jacks

Physical activity can help burn off the edge of anger, so you can think more clearly afterward.

Channel Pressure into Organization
Feeling pressure might leave you scattered. If you have a list of tasks and not enough time, it can create a whirl of stress. Try breaking the tasks into small pieces. Organize them by priority. Finishing even one small part can ease the feeling of being buried.

- **Example of Breaking Things Down:**
    1. Make a list of everything you need to do.
    2. Mark the three most urgent items.
    3. Focus on the first urgent task until it is done or until you have made progress.
    4. Move on to the next.

This structured approach often reduces pressure because you see yourself making steady progress.

Practice Saying "I Need Help"
Pressure can grow when you think you must handle everything alone. If you have

too many tasks or feel overwhelmed, consider asking for help. This could be from a coworker, a family member, or a friend. Although it might feel like a sign of weakness, asking for help can be the wise choice that prevents a meltdown.

- **Example:**
    - "I'm feeling overloaded with these tasks. Could you help me by taking over one of them?"

Check Your Energy Levels
Sometimes anger flares up when you are tired or hungry. Pressure can feel worse if you have not had enough sleep or food. Pay attention to these simple needs. If you are exhausted, get some rest if at all possible. If you are hungry, try to eat a balanced snack.

Use Calming Tools
A short calming routine can be a lifeline when anger and pressure spike. This could include:

- **Soft Sounds:** Listen to water sounds or gentle music for a few minutes.
- **Warm Cloth:** Place a warm cloth on your neck or face to ease tension.
- **Repetitive Mantra:** Repeat a phrase like "I can handle this" or "Stay calm" in your mind.

These tools act like a break for your stressed body and mind.

Avoid Quick Fixes
When anger or pressure builds, some people turn to unhealthy habits, like overeating junk food, drinking too much alcohol, or using other substances. These might mask the stress for a short time, but they do not address the root problem. In fact, they can create new problems. A healthier approach is to face the emotion directly with the methods listed here.

Find a Trusted Person to Talk To
Speaking with someone you trust can be a big relief. This might be a friend, a family member, or a counselor. Talking about your anger or pressure helps you release the emotional buildup. The other person may also share ideas or simply offer comfort. If you do not have someone close, there are hotlines or community services you can reach out to.

Set Realistic Expectations

Unrealistic expectations can cause you to feel angry or under too much pressure. For instance, if you expect people to be perfect or expect yourself to never make a mistake, you set yourself up for disappointment. Adjusting your expectations to a more realistic level can lower the chance of feeling let down.

Learn from Anger

Anger might appear because it is alerting you to something wrong or unfair. If you keep facing the same triggers, look deeper. Is there a pattern? Are there actions you can take to fix the underlying cause? Maybe you need to set boundaries or talk to someone about a recurring problem. Using anger as a signal for change—rather than a sign to explode—can be helpful.

Visualize Calm

This is a simple but powerful technique:

- **Close Your Eyes:** Imagine a place that brings you peace, like a quiet beach or a shady tree.
- **Add Details:** Picture the sounds, the air temperature, the colors.
- **Stay There Mentally:** Let yourself linger in that image for a minute or two.

Even though it is just in your mind, the act of picturing something peaceful can slow your heartbeat and steady your breathing.

Turn Anger into Motivation

Sometimes, anger can be turned into a constructive drive. For example, if you are angry about a local problem, you might volunteer or join a group that works on that issue. Channeling anger into useful action can bring a sense of purpose rather than just letting it burn inside.

Prepare for Pressured Moments

If you know certain events or people often stress you out, plan ahead. Think about steps you can take to stay calm:

- **Example:**
    - If a big exam is coming, schedule study time days in advance so you do not cram.
    - If a certain relative triggers arguments, plan ways to steer conversations to neutral topics or choose a time limit for visits.

Being ready can lessen the shock of stressful moments.

Help Someone Else
An interesting way to ease anger or pressure is to do something kind for someone else. It might seem odd, but helping another person can shift your focus away from your own stress. It could be as small as helping a neighbor carry groceries. This act often makes both people feel better.

Draw or Write Your Feelings
If speaking about your anger feels too raw, you can sketch or write it out instead. Drawing angry shapes or scribbles on paper might sound silly, but it can help you release emotion in a harmless way. Then, you could tear up the paper if you like, symbolically throwing away the negative energy.

Use Time-Outs with Family or Friends
If you live with people who also get angry, it can lead to quick flare-ups. Agree with them ahead of time to use a "time-out" system. When anyone notices the mood is getting too heated, they say "Time-out," and everyone pauses the conversation. After a few minutes, you can check if folks are calm enough to talk again.

Notice Your Triggers
Triggers are things that spark anger or pressure. Maybe it is a certain tone of voice, a messy desk, or running late. Once you know your triggers, you can be more prepared. For example, if you know that clutter makes you stressed, try spending a few minutes tidying up each morning.

Watch Out for Self-Focused Anger
People with strong self-focused habits might get angry quickly if they feel they are not getting special treatment or if they feel overlooked. If you notice this kind of anger, ask yourself whether your reaction is fair. Are you upset because something truly unfair happened, or are you simply upset that the spotlight is not on you?

Physical Relaxation Techniques
We already mentioned exercise, but there are also specific body-based methods to release tension:

- **Neck Rolls:** Gently roll your head from side to side.

- **Progressive Muscle Tensing**: Tighten a muscle group (like your fists) for five seconds, then release. Move to another group.
- **Shoulder Shrugs**: Shrug your shoulders toward your ears, hold for a moment, and relax.

Each of these can help loosen the tightness that comes with anger or heavy pressure.

Focus on Facts

Sometimes, strong feelings can lead you to make claims that are not based on reality. For instance, you might think, "Nobody ever helps me," when in fact a friend did help you last week. Instead, focus on what actually happened, not on sweeping statements like "never" or "always."

Seek Professional Guidance If Needed

If anger or pressure are controlling your life, consider getting help from a counselor or a support group. There is no shame in needing guidance. Professionals can teach you methods suited to your situation. They can also help you explore deeper issues that might be fueling your anger.

Reflect After the Storm

After an angry moment or a time of heavy pressure, look back with a calm mind. Ask yourself:

- What set me off?
- Could I have handled it in a better way?
- Did I hurt anyone with my words or actions, and do I need to apologize?

This reflection helps you learn from the experience so you can handle it better next time.

Reward Calm Actions

If you manage your anger well or cope with pressure in a healthy way, recognize that you did something good. This does not mean showing off. You can quietly acknowledge, "I stayed calm this time. That's a step forward." Keeping a mental note of these wins can build confidence in your ability to stay composed.

Summary

Anger and pressure are normal parts of life, but they do not have to control you. By spotting early signs, pausing to breathe, and choosing a helpful response, you can avoid saying or doing things you will regret. Whether it is replacing negative thoughts, using calm communication, or seeking the help of a trusted person, you have many tools to handle these strong emotions. Over time, managing anger and pressure will support the sense of calm you have been working toward.

Learning to handle anger and pressure is an important step in breaking self-focused habits. When you feel those emotions rise, you might be tempted to blame others or ignore their needs. But by using the methods in this chapter, you can respond in a way that protects your well-being and also respects the people around you. This makes it easier to keep building healthier relationships and a softer, more peaceful way of living.

Chapter 9: Building Good Boundaries

Building good boundaries means learning how to protect your personal space—both inside and out. It involves deciding what is okay and not okay in your interactions with others, and then sharing that in a clear and respectful way. Boundaries can be about physical space, like not wanting people to stand too close, or about mental and emotional areas, like not allowing people to insult you. By having solid boundaries, you can avoid many conflicts and help maintain your inner calm. This chapter will show you how to notice when your boundaries need work, ways to set healthy limits, and methods to handle situations when people push against them.

What Are Boundaries?
Think of a boundary as a protective line between you and other people or situations. It is like a fence around a yard. That fence does not keep everyone away; it just lets them know where the property line is. If someone is respectful, they will pause at the fence and ask if they can come in. If they are not respectful, they might climb over without asking.

- **Physical Boundaries:** Might include how close you allow someone to stand next to you, whether you hug someone or prefer to shake hands, or whether you let someone into your bedroom or personal space.
- **Emotional Boundaries:** Involve how much you share about your feelings or personal information and how you handle teasing or criticism. For example, if someone starts mocking your appearance, you might tell them that you do not welcome such comments.
- **Time Boundaries:** These relate to how you spend your time and whether you let others pull you away from your tasks or rest.
- **Material Boundaries:** Concern your belongings. Maybe you do not want to share your expensive tools or keep loaning money to someone who never repays you.

Why Boundaries Are Important
Good boundaries help you feel safe, calm, and respected. If you have weak

boundaries, other people might take advantage of you, whether on purpose or by accident. This can lead to resentment, stress, or even conflict. If you set extremely strict boundaries with no flexibility, you might keep everyone at a distance and feel lonely. The goal is to find a healthy middle ground.

- **Respect for Yourself:** Boundaries show that you value your own comfort and peace.
- **Respect for Others:** By setting clear limits, you also make it easier for others to know what is acceptable.
- **Better Relationships:** People who respect each other's boundaries often have fewer fights and more trust.

Common Signs You Need Stronger Boundaries

- **Feeling Drained:** If you often feel tired or stressed after being around certain people, it might be because they are crossing your boundaries.
- **Saying "Yes" Too Often:** If you find yourself saying "yes" to tasks or requests you really do not have the time or energy for, you might need firmer time boundaries.
- **Being Too Eager to Please:** When you feel uneasy about saying "no" because you fear someone will be mad or leave you, your boundaries might be too weak.
- **Frequent Anger or Resentment:** If you catch yourself thinking, "I always do things for them, but they never respect my needs," it is a strong sign your limits are not clear or enforced.

Clarifying Your Own Limits

Before you can share boundaries with others, you need to figure out what they are. Spend some quiet time thinking about moments that make you uncomfortable:

- **Physical Discomfort:** Do you feel uneasy when someone stands very close or touches you without asking?
- **Emotional Stress:** Do you dread talking about certain topics, like personal finances, with people who gossip?
- **Time Pressures:** Do you get upset when friends call or text at all hours of the night expecting immediate replies?

- **Material Concerns:** Do you feel annoyed if someone borrows your things and returns them damaged—or does not return them at all?

By identifying these issues, you can outline where your comfort zone starts and ends.

Communicating Boundaries Clearly

Once you know your boundaries, it is important to share them with the relevant people. You do not have to make a big speech; often, a simple statement in the right moment is enough.

- **Use "I" Statements:** Saying "I feel uncomfortable when…" or "I need some space right now…" sounds less accusing than "You are always doing this!"
- **Be Direct But Polite:** "I need to end our call now because I have other tasks to do." This is both honest and polite.
- **Maintain a Calm Tone:** If you sound angry, the person might become defensive. A calmer approach is more likely to lead to understanding.

Saying "No" Without Guilt

One of the hardest parts of boundary setting is learning to say "no" when you need to. It can feel rude or mean. But remember, saying "no" to something that makes you feel uneasy is a form of self-respect.

- **Short and Clear:** A simple "No, I can't do that" or "I'm not available to help with that" is often enough.
- **Avoid Over-Explaining:** You do not need to list out all the reasons why you are saying "no." A brief explanation can be helpful, but do not feel obligated to argue for your right to say "no."
- **Stay Firm if Pressed:** If the other person keeps pushing, repeat your statement. "I understand you want my help, but I'm not able to do that."

Handling Pushback

Some people might ignore or resist your boundaries. They could argue, tease, or try to make you feel guilty. This is where your resolve is tested.

- **Repeat Your Position:** Calmly say, "I've already told you that doesn't work for me."

- **Stick to Consequences:** If a boundary is broken, consider a consequence like leaving the situation or ending the conversation.
- **Know When to Seek Distance:** If someone refuses to respect your boundaries, you might need to lessen contact with them.

Physical Boundaries Examples

- **Personal Space:** If a friend stands too close when talking, you can step back or say, "Can we step back a bit? I need a little space."
- **Touch:** If relatives hug you when you are not comfortable with it, gently say, "I prefer a handshake right now," or politely hold up your hand to signal a pause.
- **Shared Living Areas:** If you share a home, you might decide that your bedroom is off-limits unless someone asks permission.

Emotional Boundaries Examples

- **Personal Topics:** If you do not want to discuss a certain issue, you can say, "I'm not comfortable talking about that."
- **Handling Criticism:** If someone criticizes you in a way that feels insulting, you can say, "I'm open to feedback, but not insults. If you want to discuss, please do it respectfully."
- **Teasing or Sarcasm:** If jokes about you feel hurtful, you can respond, "That kind of joke bothers me. Please stop."

Time Boundaries Examples

- **Work vs. Personal Time:** If you work from home and your family expects you to handle errands during work hours, you can say, "I work from 9 AM to 5 PM and can't do chores then. I'll help afterward."
- **Social Media or Phone Usage:** If friends text or call late at night, you can say, "I silence my phone after 10 PM, so I won't reply until morning."
- **Commitments:** If someone asks you to do extra tasks, but you are already busy, you can respond, "I don't have space in my schedule right now."

Material Boundaries Examples

- **Lending Items:** If people keep borrowing your stuff, you could say, "I prefer not to lend this item because I use it often."

- **Money Requests:** If someone asks for a loan and you do not feel comfortable, it is fine to say, "I'm sorry, but I'm not in a position to lend money right now."
- **Personal Belongings:** If you do not want others going through your bags or car, you can politely say, "Please ask me before you look inside my things."

Dealing with Boundary Violations

Even if you make your boundaries clear, there will be times when people do not follow them. They might forget, or they might do it on purpose. Here are ways to handle that:

- **Gentle Reminder:** "I understand you might have forgotten, but I already said I'm not okay with this."
- **Follow Through:** If you said you would leave if your boundary is ignored again, then do it. If you do not, the other person may think your boundaries are not serious.
- **Reflection:** Ask yourself if you made the boundary clear. If not, try explaining again calmly. If you were clear and they still do not respect it, you may need to limit your contact with them.

Boundaries and Close Relationships

Sometimes, it is toughest to set boundaries with the people you are closest to, like family members or dear friends. You might worry about hurting their feelings or making them upset. However, boundaries can actually improve these relationships in the long run, because they prevent silent resentment from building up.

- **Talk in a Calm Environment:** Pick a time when both of you are relaxed. Explain you care about the relationship and want it to be healthy and respectful.
- **Listen to Their Concerns:** They might also have boundaries they want to set with you. Being open to hearing them can strengthen the mutual respect.
- **Offer Reassurance:** Remind them that setting boundaries is not about pushing them away, but about making sure everyone feels safe and respected.

Boundaries with Strangers or Acquaintances

It can feel awkward to set boundaries with people you do not know well. Still, there might be times you need to do so. For instance, if a stranger on the bus is talking too closely to you, you can politely step back or say, "I'm sorry, I need a bit more space." If someone you just met asks highly personal questions, you can answer in a general way without sharing details.

Flexibility vs. Rigidity

Boundaries should be firm, but not always rigid. Some situations call for kindness or adapting a little. For example, if a close friend is in a real emergency, you might decide to let them call you after your usual "no calls" time. The key is to make sure you are freely choosing to be flexible, rather than feeling forced. If you do adjust a boundary for someone, explain it clearly so they do not assume that boundary is gone forever.

Self-Reflection and Boundaries

Setting boundaries is a skill that grows with practice. You might set a boundary and later realize it was too strong or too weak. Reflect on what happens and adjust as needed. It is also important to watch your own behavior. Sometimes, we cross other people's boundaries without noticing. By staying mindful, you can become better at respecting both your limits and the limits of others.

Emotional Fallout of Saying "No"

You might feel guilty or uneasy at first, especially if you have a habit of always saying "yes." Over time, remind yourself that caring for your peace is not selfish. A healthy boundary can prevent bigger issues, such as burnout or hidden anger. If you find it very hard to say "no," consider talking to a counselor or reading more about assertiveness skills.

Boundaries at Work or School

Work or school settings can be tricky, because you have certain obligations. Still, you have the right to say something if you feel uncomfortable. Maybe a coworker keeps asking personal questions, or a classmate teases you beyond what is acceptable. In such cases, calmly let them know their behavior is unwanted. If it continues, you may need to talk to a supervisor, teacher, or counselor.

Warning Signs of Unhealthy Boundaries

- **You Feel Bitter All the Time:** Suggests you are giving too much and not setting limits.

- **People Get Angry a Lot:** Maybe you are setting boundaries in a hostile way or you are ignoring others' boundaries.
- **You Feel Overly Isolated:** Possibly you have set boundaries so strict that nobody can get close.

If you spot these signs, do some self-checking. You may need to adjust how you share or enforce your boundaries.

Teaching Children About Boundaries

If you have kids or younger siblings, you can show them that it is okay to say "no" when they feel uneasy. Help them see they have the right to their own privacy, personal space, and property. For example, if they do not want someone to keep poking them while playing, encourage them to say, "Stop, I don't like that." This prepares them to be more assertive and respectful as they grow older.

Cultural Differences in Boundaries

Different cultures have different ideas about personal space, privacy, and manners. What feels normal in one culture might seem odd in another. Keep this in mind if you interact with people from various backgrounds. If someone seems to cross your boundary, it might be because they do not realize it. Explain gently rather than assuming bad intentions.

Boundaries and Self-Focus

Setting boundaries is an important step in moving away from harmful self-focus. Sometimes, we think of boundaries as selfish. In truth, healthy boundaries are about respect for everyone involved. When boundaries are clear, you do not have to guess how to treat each other, and you reduce the urge to control or blame others. You respect your own needs without ignoring the needs of those around you.

Encouraging Others to Set Boundaries

Sometimes, a friend or family member might struggle with saying "no." You can be a support for them by encouraging them to find what makes them comfortable. If they set a boundary with you, try to respect it without taking offense. For instance, if they tell you they need personal space, show understanding. This can inspire a healthier dynamic for everyone.

Maintaining Boundaries Over Time

Boundaries are not a one-time fix. People change, relationships change, and your comfort zones might shift. Check in with yourself regularly. Ask, "Do these boundaries still match my current life?" If you move to a new place, start a new job, or form new friendships, you may need to update or adjust your boundaries.

Overcoming the Fear of Rejection

A big obstacle to setting boundaries is the fear that someone will reject us. We might worry they will call us rude or walk away from us. While this can happen, it is also true that genuine friends and caring family will understand the need for healthy limits. If someone leaves because you set a basic boundary, it may mean they wanted to have control over you. In the long run, you are likely better off without a relationship built on that imbalance.

Practical Steps to Strengthen Boundaries

- **Write Down One Boundary You Need to Enforce:** Start small, like telling a friend to stop texting you late at night.
- **Think About the Words You Will Use:** Practice a simple sentence like, "I appreciate your messages, but I turn off my phone after 10 PM."
- **Prepare for Pushback:** The friend might say, "But I need you to be available!" Stay calm and repeat, "I'm sorry, but that time is off-limits for me."
- **Reward Your Own Effort:** (Use a modest or neutral phrase such as, "I recognize I did something good for my well-being.") This helps you get used to feeling comfortable with boundary-setting.

Boundaries in Digital Spaces

In today's world, digital boundaries matter too. People can access you by phone, social media, or email anytime. Decide who gets to see your social media posts, how quickly you respond to messages, or whether you allow work emails on weekends. If you feel overwhelmed by notifications, you have the right to turn them off or set times to check them.

Boundaries and Personal Growth

Learning to say "no" and stand up for yourself does not mean you stop caring for others. On the contrary, it can help you be more present when you choose to help. Setting a boundary lets you decide to help when you truly can, rather than feeling forced or resentful. This sense of personal choice can lead to more genuine acts of kindness.

Reflecting on Success Stories

You might think back on a time when you set a boundary and it turned out well.

Maybe you told a friend you could not talk on the phone after a certain time, and they respected it, and your friendship stayed strong. Remembering such moments can boost your confidence to keep maintaining healthy boundaries in the future.

Conclusion

Building good boundaries is not about shutting people out. It is about respecting your own comfort and teaching others how to interact with you in a balanced way. Clear boundaries reduce stress, prevent misunderstandings, and support lasting, respectful connections. Whether it is physical space, emotional needs, or time management, knowing how to voice your limits can transform your relationships—and protect your inner peace.

By learning to set and keep healthy boundaries, you take another step toward a more balanced life that values both your needs and the needs of others. In the next chapter, we will talk about handling guilt, another topic that can hold people back from feeling calm and confident. Just as good boundaries free you from unwanted burdens, addressing guilt can free you from negative feelings that come when you believe you have done wrong or disappointed others.

Chapter 10: Handling Guilt

Guilt is a feeling that arises when you believe you have done something wrong or failed to do something right. Sometimes, guilt can be healthy, reminding you to make amends if you hurt someone or broke a promise. Other times, guilt can become too heavy, causing you to feel constantly at fault, even for things beyond your control. This chapter explores how to tell the difference between helpful guilt and unhelpful guilt, and provides tools to address both. By learning to manage guilt, you can maintain healthier relationships and keep a calmer mind.

Understanding Guilt

Guilt is often linked to moral or ethical standards. You might feel guilty if you break a rule you believe in, like lying or neglecting someone you promised to help. In moderate doses, guilt can push you to correct mistakes. But guilt can also show up in times when you did nothing wrong, or when your part in the situation was very small.

- **Healthy Guilt:** Works like a signal that you might have done harm. You realize you need to fix the mistake or apologize.
- **Unhealthy Guilt:** Lingers even when you have done all you can to repair a situation. It can also appear if you blame yourself for events you could not control, like a friend's bad choice or a family member's unhappiness.

Why Guilt Matters

If managed properly, guilt can lead to personal growth. It makes you more aware of how your actions affect others. For instance, if you feel guilty for missing a friend's special event, you might try harder to be present next time. On the other hand, if guilt spirals out of control, you might start feeling you are always in the wrong. This can weaken your self-esteem and create tension in your relationships.

Signs of Unhealthy Guilt

- **Constant Apologizing:** Saying "I'm sorry" over and over, even for small things.

- **Feeling Responsible for Others' Emotions:** If someone is sad, you assume it is your fault.
- **Difficulty Accepting Forgiveness:** Even after someone forgives you, you still feel burdened.
- **Self-Punishment:** You may deny yourself fun or comfort because you believe you do not deserve happiness.

Common Causes of Excessive Guilt

- **Rigid Upbringing:** If you grew up in an environment where mistakes were not tolerated, you might believe you are bad whenever you slip up.
- **Fear of Letting People Down:** You might want everyone to be happy all the time, and feel guilty if they are not.
- **Unclear Boundaries:** If you cannot separate your responsibilities from other people's, you might take blame for things that are not truly your job to fix.
- **Unresolved Past Events:** Maybe you did something years ago that you never forgave yourself for.

Distinguishing Real Responsibility from False Guilt

Ask yourself, "Did I truly have control over the situation?" If you made a choice that hurt someone, you may have real responsibility. But if you had no direct role, your guilt might be unnecessary. For example, if a friend chooses to ignore advice you gave them and faces bad results, you are not required to feel guilty for their decision. Recognizing what is and is not your responsibility helps you be fair to yourself.

Steps to Handle Healthy Guilt

a. Admit the Mistake: If you hurt someone, own up to it without excuses.
b. Apologize Sincerely: A heartfelt apology says you regret your actions and will work to do better.
c. Make Amends: If possible, fix the situation. If you broke something, replace it. If you said hurtful words, do something kind or speak gentle words to rebuild trust.
d. Let It Go: After you have done your best to repair the damage, forgive yourself. Holding on to guilt will not help anyone.

Steps to Handle Unhealthy Guilt
a. Identify the Source: Ask, "What exactly am I feeling guilty about?" Then ask, "Is this truly my fault or just a feeling?"
b. Challenge Unrealistic Beliefs: If you believe you should never disappoint anyone, remind yourself that this is not possible—everyone disappoints someone at some point.
c. Practice Self-Forgiveness: If you are holding on to old mistakes that cannot be changed, remind yourself you did the best you could at the time.
d. Talk It Over: Sometimes, sharing your guilt with a supportive friend or counselor helps you see it more clearly. They might point out that you are being too hard on yourself.

The Role of Apologies
Apologies are useful if you have truly harmed someone. However, if you find yourself apologizing just to calm your guilt—even when you did nothing wrong—this can weaken your self-confidence. Also, constant or needless apologies can make them lose meaning when you actually have done something wrong. Try to save apologies for real mistakes, and make them genuine.

Self-Forgiveness Techniques

- **Write a Letter to Yourself:** If you feel guilty about something you did, write down what happened, what you learned, and why you forgive yourself. You do not have to show this letter to anyone—it is for your own healing.
- **Positive Affirmations:** Repeat simple statements: "I learn from my mistakes. I allow myself to move on."
- **Focus on Growth:** Instead of defining yourself by the mistake, see it as one event that taught you something. Ask, "How can I become better from this?"

When Others Use Guilt Against You
Sometimes, people might try to make you feel guilty in order to control you. They might say, "If you really cared, you would do this for me," even if what they ask is unfair. Be careful when you notice patterns like these. It might be their way of avoiding responsibility for their own actions or getting you to do things you do not want to do. If you suspect someone is using guilt against you, step back and examine the situation calmly. You might need to set firmer boundaries.

Cultural and Family Influences

In some families, guilt is a common tool. Parents might say, "I sacrificed so much for you; how can you do this to me?" This can shape how you react as an adult, making you overly sensitive to guilt. Recognizing these patterns can help you break them. You can still care for your family without letting yourself be manipulated by guilt.

Handling Guilt in Relationships

Guilt can damage a relationship if it is not addressed. For example, if you feel guilty for not meeting your partner's needs, you might start avoiding them or become clingy. On the other side, if your partner constantly blames you, you might feel guilty even when you have not done anything wrong.

- **Open Communication:** Talk about why you feel guilty. Listen to the other person's view as well.
- **Fair Requests:** Make sure you are not taking on more blame than is fair. If there is a problem, see if you both can share responsibility for a solution.
- **Forgiveness:** If both sides own up to their part, you can forgive each other and move forward with less tension.

Shifting Away from Guilt-Driven Behavior

Some people act out of guilt rather than genuine desire. For instance, you might say "yes" to every favor asked by your friend because you feel bad saying "no." But this can lead to burnout and hidden resentment. Healthy actions come from choice, not from guilt. When you decide to help, make sure it is because you truly want to, not because you are afraid of the guilt if you refuse.

Guilt vs. Shame

Guilt says, "I did something bad." Shame says, "I am bad." These are related but different feelings. Guilt can push you to fix a mistake. Shame might make you think you cannot ever be good. If your feelings are more like shame, consider talking to a counselor. Overcoming shame can require deeper self-work, because it affects how you view your entire self.

Healthy Ways to Make Amends

- **Apologize Directly:** Face-to-face if possible, or in a private message if distance is an issue.
- **Be Specific:** Say exactly what you did wrong. For example, "I'm sorry I shouted at you. I was feeling stressed, but that doesn't make it okay."

- **Ask What They Need:** Sometimes, you can fix the harm by helping. Other times, the other person only needs a heartfelt apology.
- **Respect Their Response:** They might need time to forgive or might not forgive at all. You can do your best, but you cannot force someone else to let go.

Releasing Guilt for Past Mistakes
Everyone has done things they regret—big or small. Holding on to guilt for years stops you from growing. Ask yourself, "Have I tried to correct this? Have I learned from it?" If the answer is yes, continuing to punish yourself only keeps you stuck. It might help to talk with a trusted friend or seek professional help to process deep regrets.

Handling Guilt from Self-Focused Tendencies
If you have been working on lowering harmful self-focus, you might feel guilty about things you said or did before. Recognizing past actions is good, but do not remain trapped in shame. Instead, focus on the changes you are making now. Apologize if there are people you truly hurt. Then, commit to being more caring moving forward.

Checking the Reality of the Situation
Guilt can grow if you exaggerate the harm done. Take a moment to review the facts. For instance, if you forgot to call a friend on their birthday, you might feel awful. But is it a mistake that destroys your entire bond with them, or can you send a late message or meet them to show you still care? Being realistic about the level of harm can calm overwhelming guilt.

Using Mindfulness to Spot Guilt
Guilt can sneak up on you. A mindful approach helps you notice when your mood shifts from normal to guilty. You might feel your stomach tighten or your chest get heavy. Pause and ask, "Why am I feeling this way?" Labeling the emotion can help you see if it is valid or if you are just slipping into an old habit of blaming yourself.

Outside Support
If guilt is overwhelming and you cannot seem to shake it, consider seeking professional help. A counselor or therapist can guide you through exercises to release irrational guilt and develop healthier self-talk. Sometimes, guilt stems from past experiences or deep-seated beliefs that you might need help unraveling.

Replacing Guilt with Responsibility

Instead of letting guilt weigh you down, focus on taking responsibility in a balanced way. Responsibility means you acknowledge your part and do what you can to fix it. Guilt alone can keep you stuck in negative thoughts. Responsibility leads you to a plan of action. Once you have acted responsibly, it is easier to let the guilt fade because you know you did your best.

Apologizing to Yourself

Sometimes, guilt is directed inward. You might feel you betrayed your own values or let yourself down. In such cases, think about apologizing to yourself. Write down what you wish you had done, and then write that you forgive yourself for not doing it. Promise to try a new approach next time. This can help free you from holding grudges against yourself.

Guilt and Emotional Manipulation

Be on the lookout for guilt being used as a weapon. If someone repeatedly says, "You should feel bad," or "It's your fault I'm unhappy," examine the facts. If they refuse to admit their own part in the situation, they might be trying to shift all blame to you. Healthy relationships involve shared responsibility, not one person bearing all the guilt.

Talking Guilt Out with Others

If you have a friend who understands you well, opening up about your guilt can be very healing. They might reassure you that your actions were not as horrible as you imagine or help you see a constructive path forward. Even writing an anonymous online post in a supportive forum can ease the weight, though face-to-face interaction is often more comforting.

Small Steps to Release Unneeded Guilt

- **List Out Your Worries:** Which ones do you truly control? Which ones belong to others?
- **Focus on One Area:** Choose one guilt-causing issue where you can act or apologize. Then do it, rather than staying stuck in worry.
- **Check for Over-Apologizing:** If you find yourself apologizing several times a day for small things, pause and think, "Is this really necessary?"
- **Practice Self-Compassion:** Speak to yourself as you would to a dear friend who is feeling guilty. You would not call them horrible or hopeless, so do not use those words on yourself.

Turning Guilt into Learning

After you admit a mistake, you can ask, "How can I avoid this next time?" For example, if you missed an important deadline at work, maybe you can set reminders on your phone. If you said something hurtful to a friend, you can learn to pause before speaking. Each mistake becomes a lesson, which is far healthier than drowning in guilt.

Keeping a Balanced Perspective

Being sorry for errors is part of being considerate. But it should not overshadow all your good qualities. Remember that you are more than your mistakes. Keep in mind the times you acted kindly or helped others. A balanced view of yourself includes both successes and failings, not only the failings.

Accepting That You Can't Please Everyone

A huge source of guilt is the wish to make everyone happy all the time. That is simply not possible. People have different needs, tastes, and moods. Sometimes, even a good decision can upset someone. Accepting that you cannot fulfill every wish helps you avoid guilt that arises from unrealistic expectations.

Healthy Release Rituals

If you have a symbolic way of letting go, it can help. For instance, write your guilty feelings on a piece of paper, then gently rip it up or toss it away. This physical act can represent releasing the guilt. While it might feel silly, many people find that such simple rituals help them mentally.

Conclusion

Guilt can guide you to make amends if used wisely. But when it becomes heavy and constant, it can damage your sense of self-worth and your ability to be there for others. By learning to spot the source of your guilt, distinguish healthy from unhealthy patterns, and take balanced responsibility for your actions, you can turn guilt from a burden into a signpost for growth.

Handling guilt is part of creating a healthier outlook on life. You will still make mistakes at times—that is simply being human. The important part is how you respond. Instead of sinking under guilt, face the problem with honesty, repair what you can, and then let go. This approach will keep you on track for building a calmer mind, kinder relationships, and a sense of stability that does not break every time something goes wrong.

Chapter 11: Healthy Self-Worth

A strong sense of self-worth is about seeing your own value without looking down on others or putting yourself on a pedestal. It lets you feel good about who you are, but in a balanced way that does not ignore your flaws or the worth of other people. For those who have struggled with harmful self-focus, finding healthy self-worth can help replace the constant need for praise or the fear of not being special enough. This chapter explores why self-worth matters, how to recognize signs of an unsteady sense of self, and steps to build a healthier, steadier view of yourself.

Defining Self-Worth
Self-worth is how you value yourself at your core—separate from your achievements or how others see you. When your sense of self-worth is healthy, you know you have strengths and weaknesses, yet you accept yourself. You do not need to be the center of attention, and you do not feel constant shame for being imperfect.

- **What It Looks Like:**
    1. You can handle reasonable criticism without falling apart or becoming enraged.
    2. You accept your successes with gratitude but do not see them as proof that you are above everyone else.
    3. You can forgive yourself for mistakes and learn from them.

Self-Worth vs. Self-Esteem
Some people use these terms interchangeably, but you can think of self-worth as deeper than self-esteem. Self-esteem often depends on external factors—praise from peers, good grades, or job success. Self-worth, on the other hand, stays more stable. Even if you lose a match, fail at a task, or receive criticism, you still know you have intrinsic value as a person.

- **Example:**
    1. If your self-esteem is tied to performing well at work, a demotion might make you feel like a total failure. But with a stronger sense of self-worth, you might feel disappointed

by the demotion yet still see yourself as capable and deserving of respect.

Signs of Shaky Self-Worth

- **Seeking Constant Approval:** You might crave praise and feel upset if you do not get it.
- **Putting Others Down:** If you feel unsure of yourself, you might insult others to look better.
- **Being Overly Defensive:** Even gentle feedback can trigger anger or a sense of personal attack.
- **Fear of Failure:** You might avoid new challenges because you feel your entire worth is on the line.
- **Harsh Self-Criticism:** On the flip side, if anything goes wrong, you might label yourself "useless" or "stupid."

These patterns point to a sense of worth that depends too much on outward success or on how others react. When that support is missing, it leads to insecurity.

Comparisons and Self-Worth

Comparing yourself to others too often can weaken a stable sense of self-worth. If you continually measure your achievements against someone else's, your satisfaction may vanish whenever you see someone doing "better." Instead of dwelling on what others have, focus on your own growth. Realize that each person has a different path and set of skills.

- **Example Thought Shift:**
    1. From: "They are so much more successful—what's wrong with me?"
    2. To: "I can learn from their strengths without diminishing my own abilities."

Building Self-Worth Through Honesty

A healthy view of yourself does not ignore your flaws. In fact, it starts with honest self-evaluation. You see what you do well, but you also admit your areas of weakness and your mistakes.

- **Why Honesty Helps:**
    1. It stops you from creating a false image of being flawless.

    2. It lets you work on real problems instead of pretending they do not exist.
    3. It allows you to connect with people in a more genuine way.

Self-Worth vs. Narcissism

Narcissism sometimes grows from a shaky foundation. A person might pretend they are better than everyone else to cover up hidden fears of inadequacy. When you have healthy self-worth, you do not need to broadcast your achievements or always be in the spotlight. You know you are valuable, so you feel calm even when you are not the center of attention.

- **Key Differences:**
    1. **Narcissism:** "I must be seen as the best, or I'm nothing."
    2. **Healthy Self-Worth:** "I know I have value, and so do others."

Practical Ways to Develop a Healthier Sense of Self

a. Accept Compliments Gracefully

If you tend to dismiss compliments ("Oh, it's nothing" or "I just got lucky"), practice simply saying "Thank you" and letting it sink in. This small change encourages you to believe positive feedback can be true.

b. Write Down Positive Qualities

Some people find it helpful to keep a small notebook or list of traits they appreciate about themselves—kindness, patience, creativity, or anything else. Look at this list when you feel down.

c. Learn New Skills

Trying new activities shows you that mistakes are part of learning. Each time you pick up a new skill, you gain confidence in your ability to handle challenges.

d. Track Accomplishments and Effort

Instead of only focusing on the outcome—like a grade or a prize—also note the hard work you put in. This reminds you that your worth is linked to your willingness to try, not just the final result.

Healthy Self-Talk

Words in your own mind can shape how you see yourself. If you constantly call yourself names, you invite negative feelings. Switching to gentler, more realistic language builds your sense of worth from the inside.

- **Example of Self-Talk Shift:**
    1. Negative: "I failed this test, so I'm a complete loser."

2. Positive: "I failed this test, but I'm still learning. I can study differently next time."

Handling Criticism in a Balanced Way

Criticism can be helpful or hurtful. If your sense of self is shaky, any negative remark might feel devastating. But with healthy self-worth, you can evaluate criticism to see if it is valid.

- **Steps to Handle Criticism:**
    1. Pause and take a breath instead of instantly reacting.
    2. Ask, "Is there truth to this? Could I improve in this area?"
    3. If the feedback is untrue or given in a mean way, remind yourself that not all criticism is fair.
    4. If it is fair, decide what you can change. Thank the person if the feedback was given kindly.

This approach helps you grow from honest feedback while staying steady in your sense of worth.

The Role of Forgiving Yourself

Nobody is perfect. When you make mistakes, owning up to them is good, but so is letting go of endless guilt. Forgiving yourself does not mean ignoring the impact of your actions. It means you recognize the error, try to fix it, and then allow yourself to move on. This step keeps your self-worth safe from the downward pull of shame.

Avoiding the Trap of Pride

Pride can show up when a person feels good about themselves but begins to see others as less worthy. True self-worth does not need to put others down. You can be proud of your progress without using it to feel superior. If you catch yourself thinking, "I'm better than them," remind yourself that each person has value, just as you do.

Healthy Boundaries and Self-Worth

When you know your worth, you also know you deserve respect. This means you will be more likely to set boundaries if someone mistreats you. You will not tolerate people who belittle or insult you. However, you also stay open to hearing others' opinions, because you are not threatened by simple disagreements.

Surround Yourself with Supportive People
If you spend time around people who always criticize or belittle you, it can erode your sense of self-worth. While you cannot always avoid negativity, try to build relationships with folks who treat you and others with kindness. A supportive circle can encourage a more balanced, confident view of yourself.

Self-Worth and Achievements
Achievements can give you a nice boost of confidence, but they do not define who you are at the core. If your sense of worth relies heavily on trophies, degrees, or titles, you risk feeling empty if those things are taken away. Remind yourself that your value comes from being a living, feeling person capable of compassion, creativity, and growth—achievements are just a bonus.

Admitting Weaknesses Without Losing Value
A sign of healthy self-worth is the ability to say, "I'm not good at this yet," or "I need help," without feeling worthless. This can improve relationships because you become more open to teamwork and honest communication.

- **Example:**
    - "I struggle with time management. Can we brainstorm ways to stay on track together?"

By admitting weaknesses, you give yourself room to learn. You also let others see that you are genuine, which often brings people closer.

Dealing with External Pressure
Society and social media can push ideals—like having the perfect body, a perfect home, or the perfect lifestyle. If you base your worth on matching these ideals, you may never feel good enough. Healthy self-worth stands firm even when you do not meet every expectation. You can appreciate your unique path instead of forcing yourself to match unrealistic images.

Replacing Overconfidence with Quiet Assurance
Overconfidence and genuine self-worth might look similar on the surface, but they come from different places. Overconfidence can be loud—lots of bragging or bold claims. Quiet assurance, on the other hand, does not need constant broadcasting. You trust your abilities and accept what you cannot do, and you do not constantly seek approval. This balance keeps you grounded.

Helping Others While Respecting Yourself
Having a solid sense of self-worth can improve your kindness toward others. You are more willing to offer help or support because you do not fear being taken advantage of. You also know how to say "no" when you cannot help, because you respect your own limits. You do not give out of guilt or a desire to prove your worth; you give because you genuinely want to.

Using Affirmations Wisely
Affirmations are positive statements you say about yourself. For instance, "I am worthy of respect," or "My feelings matter." These can be helpful, but they need to be grounded in reality. If you say an affirmation you do not believe at all, you might create friction inside. Choose statements that gently challenge your negative self-talk, but still feel believable enough that you can start to accept them.

Self-Worth Activities

- **Gratitude Check:** Write down three things you did today that you appreciate about yourself. Maybe you made someone smile, stayed calm under pressure, or finished a small task you had been putting off.
- **Compliment List:** Reflect on a compliment someone gave you in the past. Think about why they said it. Let yourself acknowledge its truth.
- **Kind Deeds:** Do something kind for someone else without expecting praise. Notice that you do not need applause to feel the warmth of doing good.
- **Regular Reflection:** Once a week, note an area where you see personal growth. This could be improved patience, better communication, or a new skill.

Mindfulness and Self-Worth
Mindfulness involves paying attention to the present moment without judgment. Practicing mindfulness can help you catch negative self-talk before it spirals. If you notice harsh thoughts creeping in, pause and acknowledge them. Then you might replace them with something more caring, or at least remind yourself that a single negative thought does not define your value.

Handling Setbacks with Self-Compassion
Failure can test your self-worth. Instead of seeing a setback as proof of personal deficiency, treat it as a normal part of life. Think about what you can learn. Use a

tone in your own mind that you would use with a friend. If your friend fails, you would likely comfort them, not shame them. Offer that same kindness to yourself.

When Low Self-Worth Comes from Past Experiences
Some people grew up in environments where they were not valued or were constantly compared to others. If this is the case, building self-worth might feel like an uphill task. You might consider working with a counselor to unpack those past messages and replace them with healthier beliefs. Even small steps forward can reshape how you see yourself over time.

Learning to Receive Help
People with unsteady self-worth sometimes push help away, feeling they must do everything alone to prove their value. However, allowing others to assist you can be a sign of trust and self-respect. You recognize that you are not perfect and that you do not have to be. Accepting help can also strengthen bonds with those who care about you.

Combining Self-Worth with Humility
True self-worth is compatible with humility. Humility means you realize you do not have all the answers, and you are open to learning. You do not see yourself as less than others, nor do you see yourself as more. You know your own worth while acknowledging that everyone else has worth, too. This mindset creates respect and understanding in your relationships.

Healthy Self-Worth and Empathy
When you believe in your own value, you are more likely to see value in others as well. This ties in with empathy. You understand that your needs matter, and so do the needs of the person across from you. In a conversation, you can listen better, because you do not feel a need to prove yourself all the time. Self-worth and empathy work together to form balanced, caring connections.

Watching Out for Self-Sabotage
Sometimes, when people feel undeserving, they sabotage their own success. If good things start to happen, they might break plans, quit a project, or end a relationship because deep down they feel they cannot handle the positive outcome. If you notice this in yourself, it might be a sign that your self-worth needs more support. Remind yourself you do deserve healthy relationships and achievements.

Setting Personal Goals
Goals can help boost your sense of capability. Choose goals that stretch you a little but are realistic enough to attain with proper effort. Each time you achieve a small goal, you reinforce the idea that you can trust yourself. If you do not reach a goal, view it as a clue to adjust your methods rather than a final verdict on your worth.

Embracing Your Uniqueness
A big part of self-worth is recognizing that you are a unique person with your own blend of talents, traits, and interests. You do not need to be a carbon copy of anyone else, and it is okay if your path looks different. By embracing what sets you apart, you give yourself freedom to grow without constant worry about meeting someone else's blueprint for success.

Conclusion
Healthy self-worth lets you see your own value without falling into arrogance or self-hate. It is built on honesty, self-compassion, and a willingness to learn. With a steady sense of worth, you do not crave constant attention, and you do not crumble under criticism. You can handle life's ups and downs, knowing that your value remains intact.

As you strengthen your self-worth, you will likely find your interactions with others become smoother. You no longer need to dominate conversations or hide behind an overblown image. You can be true to who you are. In the next chapter, we will look at focusing on kindness—an outlook that not only helps those around you, but also deepens your sense of peace and connection.

Chapter 12: Focusing on Kindness

Kindness is a simple concept: treating others and yourself in a gentle, helpful, and caring way. For someone working to move away from harmful self-focus, practicing kindness can shift attention toward the well-being of others without neglecting your own needs. This chapter explores what kindness looks like in day-to-day life, how it differs from people-pleasing, and practical ways to make kindness a steady habit that supports empathy and inner calm.

Understanding What Kindness Means
Kindness involves showing concern for other people's feelings and acting in ways that help or comfort them. It is not about grand gestures only; small, everyday actions also count. You might hold a door for someone, lend a hand to a neighbor, or listen attentively to a friend. Every thoughtful act builds a more caring environment.

- **Core Elements of Kindness:**
    - Respect for the other person's feelings and boundaries
    - Offering help where you can
    - Speaking with warmth and concern instead of harshness or ridicule
    - Remembering that small acts matter

Kindness vs. People-Pleasing
There is a difference between being kind and trying to please everyone at your own expense. People-pleasing often comes from fear—fear of not being liked, fear of conflict, or fear of being alone. Kindness, on the other hand, comes from genuine caring. When you are kind, you act out of empathy, not out of panic or guilt.

- **Signs of People-Pleasing:**
    - Agreeing to tasks you have no time or energy for just to avoid saying "no"
    - Changing your opinions quickly to fit in
    - Feeling you have to manage everyone's feelings to keep peace
- **Signs of Genuine Kindness:**

- You help when you can, but you say "no" when you cannot
- You do good deeds freely, not expecting constant praise in return
- You respect others' autonomy and do not try to control them

How Kindness Counters Harmful Self-Focus

A self-focused mindset often involves thinking primarily about how situations affect you. By focusing on kindness, you train your mind to also consider how your actions affect others. This shift in perspective builds empathy because you begin seeing people as individuals with their own challenges and feelings.

- **Example:**
  - Self-Focused Thought: "I'm upset the store clerk was slow—my schedule is important."
  - Kind Thought: "I wonder if the store clerk is new or having a hard day. Maybe I can be patient and friendly."

Benefits of Practicing Kindness

- **Warmer Relationships:** Acts of kindness can spark trust and closeness.
- **Reduced Stress:** When you focus on helping others in healthy ways, you spend less time ruminating on your own troubles.
- **Higher Sense of Fulfillment:** Knowing you have brightened someone else's day often leads to a sense of purpose.
- **Positive Cycle:** Kindness can prompt others to respond kindly in return, creating a loop of caring behavior.

Starting with Self-Kindness

It may sound contradictory, but being kind to yourself is essential if you want to be kind to others. Self-kindness means treating your own body and mind with care—eating well, resting, speaking to yourself gently, and seeking help if you are struggling. If you ignore your own well-being, you risk burnout or resentment that can block genuine kindness toward others.

- **Simple Self-Kindness Acts:**
  - Taking a short break when feeling overwhelmed
  - Reminding yourself it is okay to make mistakes

- Rewarding yourself with a restful activity when you finish a difficult task

Kindness in Speech

Words can either lift people up or tear them down. Think about how you speak to friends, family, coworkers, and even strangers. Are your words often critical or snappy? Or do you use a calm and caring tone?

- **Tips for Kind Speech:**
  - Pause before speaking if you feel irritated
  - Ask questions to show real interest in what the other person says
  - Give genuine compliments—something specific that shows you notice their efforts
  - Avoid gossip or making fun of others' flaws

Everyday Acts of Kindness

You do not need a big plan to be kind. Simple things can have a strong impact:

- Holding the door for the person behind you
- Giving up your seat on a bus if someone else needs it more
- Sending a text to a friend who might be feeling low
- Checking on neighbors, especially if they live alone or seem stressed

These acts might feel small, but they can build a sense of connection in a world that often feels disconnected.

Listening as an Act of Kindness

Sometimes, the kindest thing you can do is listen without judging or interrupting. Active listening is a core part of empathy, which you explored in earlier chapters. By letting someone share their worries or joys without turning the conversation back to yourself, you show that you value them as a person.

- **Practice:**
  - Maintain soft eye contact
  - Use nods and brief words like "I see" or "That sounds hard"
  - Resist the urge to rush in with "me too" stories

Kindness Beyond Your Inner Circle
It is easy to be nice to friends or family, but what about strangers, or those who seem very different from you? Reaching out with kindness in these situations can break down barriers and help you see that everyone has worth.

- **Ideas:**
  - Smile at someone in line at the store
  - Leave a small positive note in a public space (if allowed)
  - Thank service workers—like waiters or cashiers—sincerely for their help

Kindness vs. Approval Seeking
Some might do kind acts just to hear "You're so good!" However, if your main motive is to gain praise, you are leaning back toward a self-centered mindset. True kindness does not demand recognition. That does not mean you should reject appreciation. If someone thanks you, you can enjoy that moment. But let it be a bonus, not your driving force.

Balancing Kindness with Boundaries
Being kind does not mean letting people walk all over you. If someone constantly demands your help but never respects your limits, you can practice kind refusal. A gentle but firm "I'm sorry, I can't help with that right now" is honest and still respectful. You cannot be truly kind if you are resentful or exhausted because you always say "yes" out of fear.

Turning Anger into Kindness
When you feel annoyed, a quick reaction might be harsh words or anger. Instead, you can pause and choose a kind response:

- **Example:**
  - You are stuck in traffic and someone cuts you off. A typical reaction might be yelling or honking aggressively. A kinder approach: take a breath, assume maybe they are in a rush for a serious reason, and let it go. You protect your own peace and avoid escalating tension.

Kindness in Group Settings
If you are part of a team or club, you can show kindness by sharing credit, praising group members' contributions, or offering to do less glamorous tasks that need to be done. This fosters a supportive environment where everyone feels included.

Using Kindness to Strengthen Empathy
Each act of kindness creates a bridge of empathy. You start to see how your words and deeds can either help or hurt. This makes you more aware of people's feelings, which further reduces self-focused thinking. Over time, kindness and empathy can become natural parts of how you interact with the world.

Learning from Role Models
Think of someone you know who is kind. It could be a grandparent, teacher, neighbor, or community figure. Notice how they speak and behave. You can pick up cues from them—like using gentle words or offering help without making a big show of it. Role models can inspire you to bring more kindness into your daily life.

Handling Unkind Responses
Unfortunately, not everyone will respond to your kindness with gratitude. Some might remain rude or dismissive. Remember that kindness is not about controlling how others act. It is your choice to behave in a caring way. Keep showing kindness where you can, while still keeping boundaries if someone is harmful or disrespectful.

Encouraging Others to Be Kind
When you show kindness, you often inspire others to do the same. This ripple effect can be seen when a person who receives a friendly act then passes it on to someone else. You do not have to lecture others on being kind; simply do your part. Sometimes, actions speak louder than words.

Kindness and Forgiveness
Forgiveness can be one of the hardest but most powerful forms of kindness—both to others and to yourself. If a friend made a mistake and apologized, you might choose to let go of your anger. Or if you messed up in the past, you can choose to forgive your own error and move forward. Forgiveness does not mean forgetting the lesson; it means releasing the grip of resentment.

Recognizing Your Limits
If you are physically or mentally drained, you might not have the energy to help others. In that case, be honest with yourself. Take time to recharge. Kindness should not come at the cost of your own health. Taking care of yourself means you can continue to offer genuine kindness over the long run, instead of burning out and losing patience.

Kindness in Conflict Situations

A disagreement does not have to be nasty. You can stay respectful even when you disagree:

- **Tips:**
    - Avoid insults and name-calling.
    - Focus on the issue, not the person's character.
    - Listen to their viewpoint before stating your own.
    - Show you care about finding a fair solution, not just about "winning."

By keeping kindness in mind during arguments, you can often prevent relationships from falling apart over disagreements.

Kindness Toward Nature and Animals

While this book focuses on people, kindness can also extend to living creatures around you. Simple acts like not littering, recycling, or treating pets well show awareness that all living things deserve care. This broader view of kindness helps you step outside your own concerns and see your place in the larger world.

Being Kind When You Are in Pain

Sometimes you are hurting—maybe emotionally or physically—and you feel you have nothing left to give. In such moments, it can still help to be kind in small ways, even if that only means not taking out your pain on others. A calm word, a polite smile, or just letting someone pass you in a hallway can keep you from adding more negativity to your surroundings.

Kindness and Honesty

Being kind does not mean hiding the truth. If a friend is about to make a mistake and they ask for your advice, you can gently tell them your concerns. Honesty delivered with care is often more valuable than lying to avoid hurting their feelings. The difference is in how you say it—kind words look for a helpful approach, not a hurtful one.

Spreading Kindness Online

The internet can be a place of harsh comments and quick judgments. You can make a positive difference by choosing not to join in hateful discussions or rude replies. If you see someone being harassed, you can offer them a few supportive words or report the abuse if needed. You can also choose to share uplifting or informative content that helps others, instead of negativity.

Keeping a Kindness Journal
Sometimes, people forget the good things they do. Keeping a brief journal of acts of kindness (both those you do and those you receive) can encourage you. You might write down small entries like, "Gave up my seat on the bus to an older person," or "My coworker brought me a cup of tea when I was busy." These reminders show how kindness flows in both directions.

Resisting Cynicism
It can be tempting to think, "Kindness is pointless—people will just take advantage," especially if you have experienced disappointment. However, acts of kindness often have a deeper effect than you realize. While it is true that not everyone will respond positively, many do. The more people who show kindness, the more it can shape a friendlier environment for all.

Kindness and Your Mood
Research suggests that being kind can lift your own mood. You might feel a sense of warmth or satisfaction, often called a "helper's high." While this is not the only reason to do good, it does show that helping others and respecting them can also be a source of personal well-being.

Encouraging Children to Be Kind
If you have children or younger siblings, you can model kind behavior for them. Speak politely, thank them when they do something helpful, and correct them gently when they act unkindly. Praise them for showing compassion to friends, pets, or classmates. This early learning sets a foundation for empathy and consideration in their future.

Kindness in Busy Times
You might feel too busy to pause and show kindness. However, kindness often does not take much time. A quick smile or a two-sentence text can be enough to brighten someone else's day. Even scheduling one act of kindness daily—like giving a small note of thanks to a coworker—can fit into a hectic routine.

Conclusion
Focusing on kindness involves small, daily decisions to treat yourself and those around you with respect and care. It reduces self-centered habits by redirecting your attention to the needs and feelings of others, while still honoring your own boundaries. From kind words to simple favors, the effects of these acts spread in ways you might not always see, helping you and the people around you feel more connected and at ease.

Chapter 13: Releasing Harmful Thoughts

Everyone has thoughts that trouble them at times—worries, doubts, or upsetting images that linger in the mind. These thoughts can make it hard to stay focused or feel at ease. While some may fade on their own, others turn into a stubborn loop of fear or shame. Learning to release harmful thoughts allows you to regain a calmer mind and protect your well-being. This chapter explores different types of harmful thoughts, why they happen, and methods to let them go.

Recognizing Different Kinds of Harmful Thoughts
Harmful thoughts can take various shapes. Some people struggle with strong worries about the future. Others replay past mistakes again and again. Still others face unkind self-talk that tells them they are not good enough. Here are a few common types of harmful thinking:

- **Catastrophizing:** Imagining the worst possible outcome. For instance, believing that a small mistake at work means you are doomed to get fired and never find another job.
- **Black-and-White Thinking:** Seeing people or events as all good or all bad, without any middle ground.
- **Rumination on Past Errors:** Replaying an embarrassing moment or a time you said the wrong thing, and punishing yourself for it over and over.
- **Unfair Comparisons:** Constantly comparing your life or abilities to others in a way that makes you feel inferior.
- **Harsh Self-Criticism:** A mental voice that calls you names, labels you worthless, or insists that you can never change.

Recognizing what kind of harmful thoughts you often have can be the first step to addressing them. It helps you see a pattern and realize you are not alone in experiencing these mental loops.

Why Harmful Thoughts Linger
There are multiple reasons why harmful thoughts can linger:

- **Emotional Weight:** If a thought taps into deep emotions like fear, guilt, or sadness, it can remain stuck.

- **Habitual Patterns:** The mind can form habits. If you often dwell on regrets, your brain might return to those thoughts out of routine.
- **Unresolved Issues:** If there is something in your life you have not fully worked through, your mind may keep bringing it up, hoping you will address it.
- **Lack of Tools to Cope:** Sometimes, people do not know healthy ways to handle negative feelings, so the thoughts keep circling without relief.

The Impact of Holding Onto Harmful Thoughts

Keeping a tight grip on destructive thinking can affect your health, mood, and relationships:

- **Increased Stress and Anxiety:** Your body might respond with tight muscles or racing heartbeats, leading to chronic tension.
- **Lower Self-Worth:** Constant self-criticism can drain your sense of value.
- **Relationship Strains:** If you are stuck in negative thoughts, you may lash out at friends or withdraw from loved ones.
- **Lack of Focus:** It becomes harder to pay attention to school, work, or everyday tasks.

Shifting Your Perspective

Sometimes, releasing harmful thoughts involves seeing them in a different light. You can try stepping back and asking:

- "Is this thought really true?"
- "What evidence do I have that contradicts this belief?"
- "Even if this situation is not perfect, is there a more balanced way to see it?"

These questions can loosen the grip of an extreme or unfair idea. For instance, if you are thinking, "I always fail," you might remind yourself of times you succeeded. This is not about ignoring real issues but about questioning thoughts that are too absolute or too dark.

Mindful Observation of Thoughts

In earlier chapters, we discussed mindfulness as a tool for finding calm. The same approach helps with harmful thoughts. Instead of fighting them or labeling them as "bad," you watch them calmly. You imagine yourself as a spectator observing your own mind. By doing this, you give the thoughts space to arise and fade naturally, instead of chasing them away or getting lost in them.

- **Simple Mindfulness Exercise:**
    1. Sit or lie down in a quiet spot.
    2. Focus on your breathing for a few moments.
    3. When a negative thought appears, label it gently ("worry," "memory," or "fear") and let it pass by without judgment.
    4. Return your focus to your breath.
    5. If the thought keeps returning, keep labeling it each time.

Over time, this process teaches your brain that thoughts come and go. They do not have to define your actions or feelings unless you choose to act on them.

Replacing Negativity with Balanced Self-Talk

Some harmful thoughts involve harsh words toward yourself. In those moments, you can practice replacing them with balanced statements. For instance:

- **Harmful Thought:** "I'm completely useless."
- **Balanced Statement:** "I may be struggling with this task, but I have overcome other challenges before. I can learn or seek help."

This shift does not have to be overly cheerful or unrealistic. It just needs to provide a kinder and more accurate view of the situation.

Releasing Guilt and Regret

Many harmful thoughts revolve around guilt for past mistakes or missed opportunities. If you have already apologized or tried to fix a wrong, holding onto the guilt may serve no purpose other than self-punishment. You can gently remind yourself that you have done what you can, and that continuing to relive the event will not change the past. By focusing on what you can do now, you let the old guilt loosen its hold.

Using Physical Outlets

Sometimes, harmful thoughts create emotional pressure that needs an outlet. Physical activities—like taking a brisk walk, doing simple exercises, or even shaking out your arms—can release built-up tension. It can be helpful to see these movements as symbolically shaking off the negative energy. When your body feels lighter, your mind often follows suit.

Engaging in a Relaxing Hobby

If your mind is stuck in a negative loop, shifting your focus to something enjoyable can give your thoughts a rest. This might be painting, playing an instrument, baking, reading a calming book, or doing a puzzle. The goal is not to ignore your problems, but to give your brain a break so that fresh perspectives can arise. You might find that after a session of a relaxing pastime, you see your worries differently.

Talking It Out

Harmful thoughts can grow bigger in isolation. If you share them with a trusted friend, family member, or counselor, you might realize they are not as huge or frightening as they feel inside your head. Sometimes, others can offer insights or alternative viewpoints. Even if they do not have a solution, just talking can bring relief.

Journaling

Writing down what is spinning in your mind can have a freeing effect. Once your thoughts are on paper, they may not seem as overwhelming. You can also spot patterns or triggers for your harmful thinking. If you keep a journal regularly, you might discover that certain places, people, or situations spark negative loops, and then you can plan how to handle them better.

Breathing Techniques for Calming the Mind

Deep, slow breathing can be a quick way to lower the intensity of harmful thoughts. If you notice a flood of negativity, pause and do the following:

2. Breathe in for a count of four.
3. Hold your breath for a second.
4. Breathe out for a count of four.

Repeat a few times while focusing on how your chest or stomach moves. This simple practice can help break the cycle of racing thoughts and bring you back to the present moment.

Recognizing Triggers

Certain experiences or reminders might set off your harmful thoughts. For example, if you scroll through social media and see everyone's "perfect" life, you might start feeling worthless. Or if you talk to a specific person, you might leave the conversation feeling guilty or criticized. By recognizing these triggers, you can plan ways to respond differently—maybe limiting your social media time or preparing a brief polite exit when a conversation becomes too negative.

Seeking Professional Guidance
If harmful thoughts become overwhelming or lead to serious anxiety, sadness, or panic, consider seeing a mental health professional. Therapists can provide specialized techniques such as cognitive-behavioral methods. They might help you track and reframe recurring negative thoughts in a structured way. Seeking support is not a sign of weakness; it is a choice to learn better strategies for mental health.

Letting Go of Perfectionism
Perfectionism can fuel harmful thinking, as no one can meet impossibly high standards all the time. If you believe you must never fail or always please everyone, you will likely criticize yourself harshly whenever you fall short. Learning to accept "good enough" in certain areas can free you from constant mental strain. You can remind yourself that being a human means sometimes making mistakes or doing things in an average way.

Visualizing Release
Some people find it helpful to imagine placing their harmful thoughts into a balloon and letting it float away, or putting them in a box and setting that box aside. This mental picture can help you detach from the thoughts. While it may feel silly at first, visualization can be powerful because the mind responds to images and symbols. You are telling yourself, "I do not need to carry this burden around all the time."

Positive Media and Influences
The content you consume can affect your thought patterns. If you watch or read materials that constantly fuel fear or negativity, your mind may hold onto dark perspectives. Balancing that with uplifting or thoughtful content can make a difference. It does not mean you ignore reality, but you choose to feed your mind with healthier stories and knowledge.

Gradual Exposure to Fears
Some harmful thoughts are tied to fears about specific things—public speaking, for instance. Hiding from fear can make it loom larger in your mind. Gradual exposure, where you face the feared situation in small steps, can reduce its hold. If you fear speaking up in meetings, you might start by making a short comment

or asking a small question. Over time, you prove to your mind that the feared outcome is less likely or less severe than you imagined.

When Harmful Thoughts Involve Anger
Harmful thoughts are not just about fear or guilt; they can also involve anger or resentment. You might replay how someone offended you, letting the rage burn you up. While anger is a normal emotion, allowing it to grow inside can harm you more than the other person. Finding ways to cool that anger—through calming exercises, therapy, or discussing the issue—helps you move forward rather than stay stuck in bitterness.

Setting a Time Limit on Worry
One trick for people who struggle with endless worry is to schedule a short "worry time" each day. You set aside, say, 15 minutes to let your mind go over anxieties. If a worry appears at another time, you remind yourself, "I'll think about that during my worry time." This approach keeps worries contained so they do not overrun your entire day. After the set time, you close that mental door and do something else.

Reflecting on Past Successes
A big part of harmful thinking is forgetting that you have survived challenges before. If you recall times when you overcame hardships, you remind yourself you have inner strengths. Perhaps you found a job after losing one, fixed a conflict with a friend, or learned a new skill despite failing the first few tries. Reflecting on these experiences can soften the blow of negative thoughts that say you "can't handle anything."

Stopping the "What-If" Spiral
Many harmful thoughts begin with "What if?"—"What if I mess up?" "What if they reject me?" "What if everything goes wrong?" While planning can be smart, endless "what-if" scenarios might just create anxiety. Ask yourself: "What is most likely to happen based on facts?" or "Can I handle it if this goes wrong?" Often, the answer is yes, or you will find ways to cope.

Building a Support System
We are social beings. Having friends, family, or mentors you trust can act as a safety net when harmful thoughts appear. You can call or text someone who listens and reminds you of reality. You can discuss whether your thoughts are

balanced or not. Also, being supportive to others can pull you out of focusing too much on your own negative views.

Accepting Imperfection
Allowing yourself to be imperfect can help you release many damaging thoughts. You do not have to fix every error instantly or measure up to every expectation. This does not mean you stop trying to grow—it means you do not beat yourself up for normal human flaws. Accepting imperfection helps you be gentler when your mind spirals into negativity.

Capturing Thoughts and Countering Them
A technique from cognitive therapy is to write down harmful thoughts and then write a balanced counter-thought next to each one. For instance:

- **Harmful Thought:** "I will fail this new project, and everyone will see I'm incompetent."
- **Counter-Thought:** "I have completed challenging tasks before. Even if I struggle, I can seek support and learn. People generally want me to succeed."

Seeing the two side by side helps your mind grasp that the negative viewpoint is not the only possibility.

Handling Thoughts About Regret or Loss
Regrets often stem from feeling you missed something important in the past—perhaps a relationship ended or you passed up an opportunity. These thoughts can trap you in "if only" thinking. While it is normal to feel sorrow, focusing on regrets too often robs you of peace in the present. Gentle acceptance of the past and a decision to make the best of now can soothe this ache. Sometimes, creative activities or volunteering can shift your energy toward what you can still do, rather than what you have lost.

Using Humor
Laughter and humor can lighten the load of negative thinking. If a harmful thought is not intensely serious, you might poke a bit of fun at it. For example, if you have an extreme thought like, "I'll never accomplish anything again," imagine a cartoon version of that thought popping like a bubble. Humor reminds you that your mind can exaggerate.

Staying Grounded in the Present
Harmful thoughts often yank you into a distressing past or an imagined future. Grounding techniques bring you back to the "now." You can do this by:

- Naming five things around you that you can see, four you can touch, three you can hear, two you can smell, and one you can taste.
- Noticing the sensation of your feet on the floor or your back against a chair.

By tuning in to your current surroundings, you cut off the cycle of negative mental movies.

Reevaluating Your Inner Rules
Sometimes, we hold onto rules in our minds that are too rigid: "I must never show weakness," or "I have to succeed on the first try or I'm worthless." These rules fuel harmful thoughts. You can reflect on where these rules came from—perhaps childhood experiences or social pressures—and consider updating them. A kinder, more realistic rule might be, "It's okay to ask for help when I need it," or "It's normal to fail sometimes."

Conclusion: A Process, Not a Quick Fix
Releasing harmful thoughts is an ongoing practice. You may see progress in letting go of certain worries, only to find new doubts popping up later. That does not mean you have failed—it means your mind is active and always generating ideas, both helpful and unhelpful. By consistently applying the methods in this chapter—mindful observation, balanced self-talk, journaling, or seeking support—you build resilience and learn to free yourself from the grip of destructive thinking.

In the next chapter, we will shift our focus to improving the connections you have with people around you. Healthy relationships rely on open communication and mutual understanding, and letting go of harmful thoughts can free you to connect more genuinely with others. When your mind is not trapped in negativity, you have more space to offer support and receive it, forming bonds that enrich your life rather than drain it.

Chapter 14: Improving Connections

Strong, positive connections with others can bring meaning and comfort to your life. Whether these connections are with friends, family, coworkers, or neighbors, having healthy bonds contributes to a sense of belonging and warmth. However, for those who have struggled with self-focused habits or harmful thoughts, building these connections might feel challenging. This chapter explores ways to enhance the closeness, trust, and understanding you share with the people around you.

Why Connections Matter
Human beings are social creatures. Even if you are introverted, you still benefit from meaningful relationships. Good connections can:

- **Offer Support During Hard Times**: Having someone who listens can ease stress and provide fresh viewpoints.
- **Boost Happiness:** Laughter, shared experiences, and warmth with others brighten life.
- **Encourage Growth:** Close bonds often help us see our blind spots and push us to become kinder, more open, and more thoughtful.

While you do not need a huge network to be fulfilled, a few deep, supportive relationships can make a huge difference.

Overcoming Self-Centered Barriers
A person with very strong self-focus might talk mainly about their own needs, ignoring others' struggles. This can cause frustration or distance in relationships. If you have noticed such patterns in yourself, you can shift by:

- **Asking More Questions**: Show interest in other people's feelings and stories.
- **Listening Without Interrupting**: Let them complete their thoughts before you respond.
- **Checking Your Motives**: If you give advice or help, is it to look impressive, or is it because you truly want to support them?

Paying Attention to Nonverbal Signals

Communication is not just about words. Your facial expressions, tone of voice, and posture send strong messages. Also, other people's nonverbal cues can hint at how they feel. If someone hesitates or avoids eye contact, they might be uncomfortable or shy. Paying attention to these signs lets you respond kindly. For instance, if you see a friend slouching and speaking softly, you might ask if everything is okay or offer a comforting remark.

Showing Appreciation

When someone does something nice for you, acknowledging it strengthens your bond. This can be as simple as saying, "I really appreciate your help today" or "Thank you for listening when I was upset." Genuine gratitude makes people feel valued and more eager to continue supporting you.

- **Small Ways to Show Appreciation:**
  - Send a brief message of thanks or a thoughtful note.
  - Bring a small treat, if appropriate, as a token of gratitude (like a simple snack at work).
  - Remember significant events in a friend's life and check in—like after a big exam or a medical appointment.

Being Honest and Real

Closer connections often rely on truthfulness. This does not mean revealing every secret, but sharing your real emotions and thoughts when appropriate. If you hide your problems under a mask of "I'm fine," people may not know you need help or that you want to bond on a deeper level. Similarly, offering genuine feedback kindly can build trust. For example, telling a friend, "I'm concerned about how exhausted you seem," can open a path to mutual understanding.

Practical Listening Skills

Good listening is at the heart of building strong connections. You can practice these steps:

- **Focus:** Put away your phone and avoid other distractions while someone is talking.
- **Ask Clarifying Questions:** "How did that situation make you feel?" or "Can you tell me more about that?"

- **Reflect Back:** Summarize what they said in your own words, to show you understand. For instance, "So you felt let down when your coworker canceled the project?"
- **Avoid Half-Listening:** If you are already thinking of your next response, you might miss key points in their story.

Finding Common Ground

People connect strongly when they discover shared interests or experiences. This could be a hobby, a favorite type of music, a mutual friend, or a common goal like volunteering. Talking about shared passions can create a natural bond. You do not have to force it—just keep an open mind and notice things you both enjoy or care about.

Respecting Individual Differences

Even close friends or family members will not agree on everything. Respecting differences is crucial for keeping a healthy connection. If you disagree on a topic, focus on understanding why the other person feels that way instead of immediately trying to change their mind. You can say, "I see that this is important to you. Could you explain more about how you reached that view?" This approach usually keeps the conversation respectful, even if you do not align perfectly.

Handling Conflict Calmly

Conflict is normal in relationships. What matters is how you handle it. Yelling or name-calling can create wounds that take a long time to heal. Instead, aim for calm communication:

- **Cool Down if Necessary:** If emotions run high, ask for a short break.
- **Use "I" Statements:** "I feel upset because I thought we had plans, and then you canceled at the last minute." This approach avoids blaming the other person's character.
- **Focus on Solutions:** Ask, "How can we fix this problem in a way that works for both of us?"

When conflict is managed kindly, it can actually deepen trust, because both parties see that they can work through disagreements without tearing each other down.

Building Connections at Work or School

Your workplace or school can be a major part of life. Forming positive relationships there helps reduce stress and increases a sense of belonging. You can:

- **Show Courtesy and Helpfulness:** Volunteer when appropriate, or share resources.
- **Give Credit:** If you collaborate on a project, acknowledge the others' contributions publicly.
- **Avoid Gossip:** Speaking poorly about someone behind their back can harm trust.
- **Check In:** If a classmate or coworker seems stressed, a gentle "Are you doing okay?" can open a door to support.

Connecting Through Shared Activities

Doing things together often builds stronger ties than just chatting. That might involve:

- **Team Sports or Group Hobbies:** If you like painting, join a group class or local workshop.
- **Volunteer Projects:** Working side by side for a charitable cause helps you see the caring side of others.
- **Community Events:** Festivals, clean-up days, or local gatherings can introduce you to people who live nearby.

Shared activities create experiences you can talk about later, forming shared memories that build closeness.

Strengthening Family Bonds

Family relationships can be very supportive, but they can also carry old baggage. Improving connections with parents, siblings, or extended relatives might take patience. Some ideas:

- **Let Go of Ancient Grudges:** If you are holding onto a small resentment from many years ago, consider releasing it or discussing it respectfully.
- **Set Boundaries if Needed:** If a family member's behavior is hurtful, kindly explain what is acceptable and what is not.
- **Plan Low-Key Gatherings:** Simple family meals or walks can lead to natural conversation.

- **Offer Help:** If a family member is facing a challenge, a small act of support can reopen lines of communication.

Upgrading Your Friendship Approach

Friendships sometimes fade if you do not nurture them. If you want to deepen bonds, you could:

- **Reach Out First:** Do not wait for the friend to start every conversation. Send them a quick note to ask how they are doing.
- **Show Curiosity About Their Life:** Remember details they have shared and ask for updates.
- **Make Time:** Friendships need shared moments. Even a short phone call or an hour together can keep the bond fresh.
- **Balance Give and Take:** Make sure you are not always the one venting or always the one giving advice. Aim for mutual support.

Stepping Out of Your Comfort Zone

If you feel shy or self-conscious, reaching out might be uncomfortable. However, small steps can help. Try smiling at a neighbor, joining a casual meetup, or attending a club that interests you. Each positive interaction can boost your confidence that people do welcome your presence.

Respecting Privacy and Autonomy

Some individuals prefer to keep certain parts of their lives private. If a friend or family member does not want to talk about a certain topic, respect that. Pushing them to reveal more than they feel comfortable with can harm trust. Over time, as they see you respect their boundaries, they might open up more voluntarily.

Offering Constructive Encouragement

Encouragement can strengthen connections, but it needs to be genuine and not pushy. For instance, if a friend is attempting a new skill, you can say, "I've noticed how hard you are working on this. Your progress is clear." Avoid forcing them to do things your way. Encourage them to grow while respecting their pace.

Exploring Deeper Conversations

Bonding often grows from sharing personal stories, hopes, and fears. If you always stick to small talk, you may never reach a deeper sense of connection. You might take a gentle step by asking, "What have you been thinking about lately?" or "Has anything inspired you recently?" The key is to listen openly when they respond, without mocking or judging their thoughts.

Connecting Across Differences
In today's world, people can be divided by age, culture, or beliefs. You can build bridges by showing respect and interest in others' backgrounds. Ask questions about their traditions or viewpoint, and share your own politely if they are interested. You might not always agree, but you can still treat each other with kindness.

Maintaining Long-Distance Connections
Many relationships occur over long distances due to work, study, or family moves. You can keep these bonds strong by scheduling regular calls, video chats, or messages. Small updates about daily life—like sharing a photo of a meal you cooked—can help you feel closer despite the distance. Handwritten letters or postcards can also add a personal touch.

Giving Space for Others to Grow
People change over time. A childhood friend may develop new interests, or a sibling may adopt different life goals. While it can be jarring, try to allow room for these changes. Rather than clinging to how they "used to be," show support for their new directions and stay open to learning about their evolving interests.

Letting Humor Strengthen Bonds
Laughter can bring people together, as long as it is not at someone's expense. Sharing light-hearted moments—funny stories or humorous observations—helps form positive memories. When a friend sees that you can laugh with them (not at them), it often fosters a sense of safety and joy in the relationship.

Giving Compliments with Care
Compliments can brighten someone's day, but try to focus on more than looks. Compliment their creativity, problem-solving skills, or kindness. For example, "I admire how patient you were in that tough situation" can mean more than "Nice shirt." Genuine compliments on personal qualities or actions can deepen respect between you and the other person.

Accepting Constructive Feedback
Close connections may involve receiving feedback about your own behavior. If a friend or partner says, "I felt hurt when you canceled at the last minute," try not to be defensive. Instead, listen, apologize if you see you were at fault, and work on a better approach next time. Accepting feedback helps relationships grow.

Repairing Damaged Bonds

If you have a connection that suffered due to harsh words or misunderstandings, there might still be hope to repair it. This requires honesty, apologies, and a willingness to move forward differently. Both sides should express what they need to feel safe and respected. A single meeting may not fix everything, but it can open the door to gradual healing if both sides truly want it.

When to Let Go

Not every relationship is meant to last. If someone repeatedly disrespects you, breaks your trust, or refuses to meet you halfway, it might be necessary to let that connection fade or at least set stronger boundaries. Letting go can hurt, but it can also free you to invest in healthier bonds. The main point is not to force a relationship that has become destructive or harmful.

Connecting with Yourself

Oddly enough, improving connections with others can start with knowing yourself better. If you understand your own triggers, dreams, and emotions, you can share them clearly. You can also recognize when you need quiet time. By being in tune with yourself, you avoid blaming others for misunderstandings that arise simply because you have not sorted out your own feelings.

Volunteering for Broader Connections

Helping in your community or volunteering for a cause can connect you with like-minded people who care about the same issues. This broader sense of connection can remind you that you are part of a web of supportive individuals who work toward the common good. It also gives you a chance to practice empathy on a wider scale.

Building Trust Gradually

Trust does not form instantly. It grows as people prove themselves to be reliable, honest, and considerate over time. Keep promises you make, and do not promise more than you can deliver. If you slip up, own your mistake and fix it if possible. Little by little, these actions create a foundation of trust that can weather conflicts or misunderstandings.

Taking Time for Fun and Shared Laughter

Deep talks and serious support are essential, but so is fun. Spending time simply enjoying lighthearted moments—playing games, watching a movie, or walking in a park—adds dimension to your bonds. Laughter is often a glue that keeps relationships strong through life's ups and downs.

Conclusion: Growing Together

Improving connections requires patience, openness, and genuine interest in others. As you move away from self-focused habits, you create space in your heart and mind for the feelings, stories, and insights of the people around you. Through balanced communication, honesty, respect for differences, and readiness to handle conflict calmly, you can form and maintain bonds that bring warmth to your daily life.

Just as releasing harmful thoughts can free your mind, improving connections can free your heart to give and receive care. A strong network of supportive relationships offers comfort, encourages personal growth, and provides opportunities to show kindness. As you keep refining your ability to listen, empathize, and share with others, you will likely see your entire life become richer and more peaceful, guided by a healthier view of both yourself and the people around you.

Chapter 15: Responding to Criticism

Criticism is feedback that points out what someone thinks you are doing wrong or could do better. Sometimes, it can be delivered in a helpful way; other times, it can feel harsh or unfair. Learning to respond well to criticism helps protect your sense of calm and supports healthier relationships. Instead of seeing every critical remark as a personal attack, you can learn to see it as information—maybe it is correct, maybe it is not, or maybe it is partially right. This chapter explains why people criticize, how to handle both helpful and hurtful feedback, and practical steps to stay steady when others point out your mistakes.

Understanding Why People Criticize
There are different reasons why someone might criticize you:

- **Genuine Care:** They want to help you improve. For example, a teacher might point out errors so you can correct them.
- **Personal Frustration:** They might be dealing with their own problems and take it out on you.
- **Misunderstanding:** They could be missing key facts about your situation.
- **Desire for Control:** Some people use criticism to feel powerful, putting others down to raise themselves up.

Knowing these possibilities can help you respond in a calm, thoughtful way rather than becoming defensive.

Separating Helpful Criticism from Insults
Not all criticism is the same. Helpful criticism aims to fix a problem or guide you toward better results. Insults or harsh remarks, on the other hand, might come from anger or spite, with no intention to guide you constructively.

- **Helpful Criticism Example:**
  "I noticed you often turn your work in late. You might do better if you plan your tasks earlier."
- **Unhelpful Criticism Example:**
  "You're hopeless. You can't get anything right."

Recognizing the difference lets you focus on improving where needed and ignoring comments meant to hurt you.

Why Responding Calmly Matters
When you react with anger or shame, you might miss the useful parts of the criticism. You also risk harming your relationships. A calm response shows maturity and can even turn a tense moment into a chance to build respect. If the other person meant well, they will see you are open to growth. If they did not mean well, your calm tone can defuse their negativity.

Checking Your First Reaction
Your first reaction to criticism might be to defend yourself or to blame the other person. This is normal. However, you can train yourself to pause:

- **Take a Breath:** A slow inhale and exhale can stop an emotional outburst.
- **Step Back Mentally:** Remind yourself, "I don't have to react instantly. I can wait a moment to understand."
- **Ask for Clarification if Needed:** If the criticism is unclear, say, "Can you explain what you mean?"

These steps buy time so you can respond thoughtfully instead of snapping back.

Listening with an Open Mind
It might be tempting to tune out criticism, especially if it feels painful. But if you stay open, you might find points worth considering. To listen effectively:

- **Look at the Person:** Maintain simple eye contact if it feels appropriate.
- **Avoid Interrupting:** Let them finish before you speak.
- **Restate in Your Own Words:** Once they are done, say, "So you think I could improve by doing X?" to ensure you understand.

This approach does not mean you have to accept all they say—it just means you are taking the time to hear them fully.

Deciding If the Criticism Is Valid
After hearing someone out, ask yourself:

- "Is there any truth in what they are saying?"

- "Do I see this behavior in myself?"
- "Have I received similar feedback before?"

If the criticism seems valid, it can be a chance to correct a mistake or learn something new. If it seems off-base, remind yourself that not every opinion is accurate. Sometimes, you may find a piece of truth inside an otherwise unfair remark. For example, a coworker might deliver criticism rudely, but still point out a genuine mistake you made.

Handling Fair Criticism

When you realize the criticism has merit, you can:

- **Admit the Error:** A simple, "You're right, I see that now," can show you are responsible.
- **Apologize if Necessary:** If your action hurt someone, a sincere apology can mend trust.
- **Ask for Advice:** If the critic might help you improve, say, "I want to fix this. Do you have suggestions?"
- **Plan a Next Step:** Decide one small thing you can do to change. This shows you take the feedback seriously and want to improve.

Handling Unfair Criticism

If you conclude the criticism is unfounded, you do not have to pretend it is valid. Still, you can respond politely:

- **Remain Calm:** Anger can escalate the situation.
- **State Your View Gently:** "I understand your point, but I see it differently because…"
- **Provide Facts If Helpful:** If you have evidence that contradicts their claim, share it without being hostile.
- **Know When to End the Discussion:** If they keep pushing a wrong point, you might say, "Let's agree to disagree," and move on.

Turning Criticism into Growth

Even if you do not agree with everything, consider whether there is a small hint you can take away. Maybe their main claim was incorrect, but they noticed something you had overlooked. By scanning each critique for any gem of truth, you turn a negative moment into a path for growth. This keeps you from dismissing all criticism out of pride or fear.

Responding to Public Criticism

Sometimes, criticism happens in front of others—at work meetings, on social media, or during family gatherings. This can feel more intense because you might worry about how you look in front of the group. The same rules apply: stay calm, listen, and decide if the feedback is valid. If it is, you can say, "I see your point and will work on that." If it is not, politely correct them without belittling them.

- **Example:**
  If a coworker publicly says you forgot an important email, but you have proof you sent it, calmly say, "I understand the concern. I did send it on Tuesday at 3 PM. I can forward it again if needed." This shows confidence, clarity, and respect.

Managing Emotionally Charged Criticism

Criticism can sting more when it touches on personal fears or insecurities. For instance, if you already feel unsure about your skills in a certain area, even a mild remark can feel like a personal attack. In that moment, try:

- **A Short Pause:** Before replying, acknowledge your feelings: "Yes, I feel upset, but I can handle this."
- **Self-Soothing Words:** Remind yourself, "One person's opinion does not define me."
- **Deciding Your Reply:** If you are too emotional to speak calmly, you might say, "I'd like to talk about this later," and return to the topic once you settle down.

What to Do If You Always Take Criticism Hard

Some people feel deep shame or anger at even small suggestions. This might come from past experiences where you felt judged or ridiculed. If you notice you overreact often, you can:

- **Reflect on the Past:** Ask yourself if childhood or past events make you extra sensitive.
- **Practice Self-Validation:** Remind yourself of the good you have done so that one negative comment does not overshadow everything.
- **Seek Support:** Talking with a counselor or trusted friend can help you handle feedback more calmly.

Dealing with Constant Critics

In some cases, you might have a boss, family member, or friend who criticizes almost everything you do. This can wear you down. You can:

- **Set Boundaries:** If their remarks are truly harmful, limit how often or how long you talk to them.
- **Look for Motives:** Perhaps they are unhappy with themselves or going through stress. Knowing this can help you take their words less personally.
- **Choose What to Absorb:** Let repeated harsh comments flow past you if there is no real value in them.

Giving Yourself Permission to Disagree

Not all criticism is useful. You are allowed to decide that a certain piece of feedback does not align with your goals or values. For instance, if someone criticizes your hobby by saying it is "a waste of time," but you find joy and growth in it, you do not have to change. You can accept that they have a different view while you keep doing what matters to you.

When Criticism Turns to Bullying

Criticism crosses a line if it becomes repeated personal attacks meant to hurt you. This is not feedback—it is bullying. In such cases:

- **Stand Firm:** Calmly state that the remarks are unacceptable.
- **Seek Help If Needed:** Talk to a manager, teacher, or another authority figure if you cannot resolve it alone.
- **Protect Your Well-Being:** Sometimes, the only answer is to distance yourself from that person.

How to Apologize if You Lashed Out

If you responded badly to criticism—maybe you yelled or insulted the other person—you can still fix the damage:

- **Admit Your Mistake:** "I'm sorry I snapped at you. I was upset, but I shouldn't have spoken that way."
- **Explain Briefly (Without Excuses):** "I felt attacked and got defensive, but it was wrong to raise my voice."
- **Offer to Discuss Calmly:** "I'd like to hear your concerns again when I'm calmer. Are you open to that?"

This shows accountability and can heal relationships after a heated moment.

Using Criticism to Strengthen Bonds

Believe it or not, criticism can bring people closer if handled respectfully. When someone points out an error gently and you respond with thanks instead of anger, trust grows. They see that you value honesty, and you see that they care enough to help you improve. Over time, this can lead to deeper respect on both sides.

Criticism in Different Cultures

In some places, open criticism is common and direct. In other places, people might hint at problems indirectly. Understanding cultural differences can guide your response. If you find the style of criticism harsh, it might be normal in that environment and not meant to offend. If you move to a place with different norms, take time to learn how people usually share feedback.

Staying Confident Amid Criticism

A single critical remark can make you doubt yourself if you do not have a stable sense of worth. Remember that mistakes or flaws do not erase your overall value. You are not just the sum of your errors. Keep a mental list or journal of your strengths—times you helped someone, tasks you completed well, or positive traits like patience or humor. Revisiting these reminders can keep you grounded when someone criticizes you.

Criticism in Close Relationships

Criticism from a spouse, sibling, or best friend can hurt more because you care about their opinions. Aim for calm, open communication:

- **Assume Good Intent (If Reasonable):** Start by thinking they might want to help, not harm.
- **Keep the Tone Respectful:** If you sense a fight forming, propose a short break.
- **Agree on Possible Solutions:** Talk about what change, if any, is needed. Make sure you both have a voice in deciding the next step.
- **Give and Take:** Sometimes you might receive criticism, sometimes you might give it. Mutual respect is key.

Learning to Ask for Criticism

If you truly want to grow in a skill or habit, you can ask someone you trust for feedback. This proactive approach can reduce the shock of unexpected criticism.

For example, you could say, "I'm working on my presentation skills. Could you watch me practice and tell me what you see?" By inviting this input, you show that you are open to improvement, and you have control over the context in which you receive it.

Not All Criticism Deserves a Response
There may be times when a stranger or a random internet commenter critiques you harshly. If their opinion is not meaningful to your life or your goals, you can choose not to engage. Arguing with every critic you meet can drain your energy. Use your judgment to decide which criticisms are worth discussing and which you can simply let pass.

Handling Self-Criticism
Sometimes, you might hear an internal critical voice. This self-criticism can be even harsher than what others say. If you are constantly putting yourself down, try:

- **Identifying the Voice:** Notice when you start calling yourself names or tearing yourself down.
- **Questioning It:** Ask, "Is this true? Am I really that bad?"
- **Replacing It:** Offer a calmer view: "I made a mistake, but I can learn from this."

You can also talk to a friend or counselor if self-criticism is persistent.

Examples of Polite Responses
Here are a few short phrases you can keep in mind when someone criticizes you and you want to keep things positive:

- "Thank you for letting me know. I'll think about that."
- "I see your point; let me see how I can apply that."
- "I appreciate your feedback. I'll consider what works best in my situation."
- "I'm not sure I agree, but thank you for sharing your view."

Using polite responses encourages respectful dialogue rather than angry exchanges.

When Criticism Affects Your Confidence
After receiving strong criticism—maybe at work or from someone close—you might feel shaken. Take a moment to recover:

- **Remember Past Successes:** Think of things you have done well, so you do not lose perspective.
- **Seek Reassurance (If It Helps):** Talk with someone who can remind you of your strengths.
- **Set a Plan to Improve:** If the criticism was fair, outline clear steps to address it so you feel in control.

This approach prevents you from staying stuck in self-doubt.

Turning Criticism into a Skill-Building Tool
With a strong mindset, you can use criticism as a learning resource:

- **Note the Specifics:** If someone says you need to be more organized, ask them for specific examples or suggestions.
- **Find Resources:** If the feedback points out a gap in your knowledge, look for courses or articles that can help you grow.
- **Track Progress:** If you make a plan to improve, check in with yourself or a mentor later to see if you have made changes.

This turns critiques into a roadmap for getting better at what you do.

Helping Others Respond to Criticism
If you see friends or family struggling with criticism, you can share some of these techniques. Remind them to stay calm, look for facts, and decide if the feedback is fair. If it is fair, they can use it to improve; if it is not, they can let it go. Offer to role-play with them if they want practice responding politely to tough remarks.

Criticism vs. Boundaries
Sometimes, people might say they are "just giving criticism" when they are actually stepping all over your personal space. If they comment about your private matters in a rude way, you are allowed to say, "This topic is not up for discussion." Setting boundaries around what kind of criticism you will or will not accept can protect your emotional well-being.

Reflecting After the Moment
Once the conversation is over, you can reflect:

- "Did I handle that calmly?"
- "What can I do better next time?"

- "Is there something valuable in what they said?"
- "Do I feel proud of how I spoke, or do I need to apologize to someone?"

Over time, this habit of reflection will sharpen your ability to handle criticism smoothly.

Conclusion

Responding to criticism is an art that blends self-confidence, open-mindedness, and calmness. While some criticisms can be unfair or delivered harshly, learning to pause, listen, and evaluate can open doors for growth. By adopting polite responses, identifying what is useful, and ignoring what is not, you protect your peace and even strengthen relationships. As you practice these methods, you will notice criticism losing its power to upset you. Instead, it becomes one more source of information—sometimes helpful, sometimes not—that you can handle with steady composure.

Criticism will always be a part of life, whether in the workplace, among family, or from strangers. If you stay focused on becoming a better person rather than proving you are always right, you transform these tense moments into learning opportunities. This balanced approach also fits well with the other steps in this book, such as practicing empathy and setting boundaries. By weaving these ideas together, you develop a calmer, more respectful style of communication that nurtures healthy connections instead of harming them.

Chapter 16: Looking Past Your Own Needs

Balancing your own needs with the needs of others is a key part of overcoming harmful self-focus. While self-care and self-respect are important, an overemphasis on "me" can lead to strained relationships and missed chances to support those around you. This chapter explores ways to expand your focus to include what others need, why this does not mean ignoring yourself, and simple actions that help you become more outward-looking in a healthy, sustainable way.

Why Look Beyond Your Own Needs?
Having a life that revolves solely around yourself can limit your growth and keep you from forming deeper bonds. When you consider others—friends, family, coworkers, neighbors—you:

- **Foster Empathy:** Seeing the world through another person's viewpoint helps you understand them better.
- **Build Stronger Ties:** People often feel closer to someone who genuinely cares about their well-being.
- **Find Greater Purpose:** Helping others or participating in shared tasks can bring a sense of meaning beyond personal gain.

Looking beyond yourself also eases the pressure to be perfect or always the center of attention. You can find calm in knowing you are part of a broader community.

What It Does NOT Mean
Expanding your focus does not mean ignoring yourself. You do not have to push aside your health, happiness, or goals to meet everyone else's requests. Rather, it is about a thoughtful balance:

- **Self-Respect + Respect for Others:** You look after your needs while also noticing how you can help or support others.
- **Saying "No" When Needed:** You still maintain boundaries and do not let others take advantage of you.
- **Avoiding Overload:** If you run yourself ragged trying to fix every problem, you risk burnout.

The goal is to shift from "me first in all things" toward "we can both matter."

Seeing People as Individuals
A self-focused mindset might treat others as minor players in your own drama—people who are there to meet your needs, offer praise, or do favors. Looking beyond yourself means seeing each person as a complete individual with their own hopes, worries, and joys.

- **Ask Questions:** If you notice someone seems distracted, ask how they are doing.
- **Remember Details:** If a friend mentions a big test or job interview, check back later to see how it went.
- **Show Genuine Interest:** Instead of waiting for them to stop talking so you can share your own story, truly listen to theirs.

Shifting from "What's in It for Me?"
In many situations—like group projects or community events—you might ask, "What do I get out of this?" While that is not a bad question, always focusing on your personal gain can limit teamwork and empathy. Try adding, "How can I contribute? How can this be good for the group?" This mental shift can improve cooperation and reduce tension.

- **Example:**
  If your workplace is organizing a volunteer day at a local shelter, you could think, "I won't get paid for that, so why bother?" Or you could think, "It will help the shelter, and I will learn more about my teammates in a different setting." This new perspective makes the event more meaningful.

Respecting Other People's Time
One sign of harmful self-focus is expecting others to drop everything to suit your schedule. Maybe you demand immediate replies to your messages or assume a friend will cancel their plans to help you. Looking beyond your own needs means understanding that other people have demands on their time as well. They cannot always accommodate you instantly.

- **Practical Steps:**
  - Ask if it is a good time before you share a long story or request help.

- Offer possible time windows when planning an event, not just the one that fits you.
- Thank people for their time or effort—do not act like it is owed to you.

Choosing Compassion Over Judgment

Sometimes, you might find yourself judging others' problems as "not that big of a deal." But what is minor to you might feel huge to them. Looking beyond yourself means recognizing that someone else's pain is real to them, even if you do not relate to it personally. Compassion invites you to respond with patience and kindness rather than dismissing their struggle.

- **Example:**
  If your friend is stressed about a presentation, and you think "That's easy—why are they panicking?", pause and see it from their angle. Maybe they have anxiety about public speaking. By acknowledging this, you can show empathy instead of brushing them off.

Learning from Others

When you are self-focused, you might miss lessons you can gain from other people's experiences. Everyone around you has gone through challenges, developed skills, or learned life lessons that might help you if you pay attention.

- **Ask About Their Stories:** Find out how they solved a tough problem.
- **Observe Their Strengths:** Someone might be great at staying calm under pressure. You could ask how they developed that trait.
- **See Them as Mentors or Guides:** Even younger people can teach you something new if you listen well.

Small Acts of Service

Helping others in little ways can shift your focus outward. These do not need to be grand gestures. For instance:

- Offering to pick up coffee for a coworker who is stuck at their desk
- Sending a caring text to a friend who seems down
- Helping set up chairs at a community event without being asked

Each small act builds a habit of caring. These actions not only assist the other person but also remind you that you are part of a shared community.

Teamwork Mindset
In group projects—whether at work, school, or among friends—a self-centered approach might focus on personal credit or ensuring you look good. A teamwork mindset recognizes shared goals:

- **Give Others a Chance to Lead:** If you always take charge, step back and let someone else guide.
- **Share Praise:** When the group succeeds, highlight everyone's contributions, not just your own.
- **Help Quiet Voices:** If someone in the group is shy, invite them to share their ideas.

Learning to Delay Your Own Comfort
Sometimes, looking past your needs means waiting a bit before satisfying your own wants. For instance, if a task benefits many people but inconveniences you slightly, you might choose to accept that inconvenience. This skill can be practiced in small ways, such as letting someone with fewer items go first in the store checkout line. It trains you to see beyond your immediate preference.

Balancing "Me-Time" with "We-Time"
You still need to protect your own well-being, so you are not expected to become a self-sacrificing doormat. A healthy approach might include:

- **Designated Personal Time:** Maybe you keep an hour each day for yourself—reading, a walk, or simply resting.
- **Shared Time:** In your free hours, look for ways to connect with friends or family, helping or just enjoying each other's company.
- **Clear Communication:** If someone asks for more than you can give, politely explain your limits. That way, you stay balanced and do not burn out.

Noticing Others' Nonverbal Cues
Many people do not always voice their needs. They might show signs of stress or sadness through their posture, facial expression, or lack of energy. If you pick up on these signals, you can gently ask if they want to talk. This attention to subtle clues shows you are tuned into their well-being, not just waiting for them to speak about your interests.

Sharing Resources

Sometimes, you have knowledge or items that could help someone else. A self-focused person might keep everything to themselves. But if you have, for example, a useful book, a spare tool, or an extra seat in your car, offering it to someone in need can brighten their day. It also builds trust, because they see you as someone who is willing to share without expecting something in return.

Encouraging Others' Success

A strong self-focus can lead to envy or resentment when someone else does well. But looking past your own needs lets you cheer for others. You realize there is room for many people to shine. When a friend reaches a milestone or a coworker gets recognition, you can show genuine happiness for them. This positive energy often returns to you in the form of mutual support.

Watching Out for Self-Praise

Sometimes, people do good deeds but then brag about them nonstop. That can become another form of self-focus, where helping others is just a way to get applause. True outward focus aims to assist without constant demands for praise. You can still feel good inside about doing the right thing, but you do not need to broadcast it to prove your worth.

Inviting Others' Opinions

If you always make decisions alone, you might miss valuable input. Asking what others think shows respect and also opens doors to better solutions. For example, if you are planning a group outing, let the group share ideas. If you are at work, ask your team what they think about a new process. Hearing their thoughts might improve the outcome while showing you respect everyone's viewpoint.

Avoiding the "Hero" Complex

While it is good to help, be careful not to become someone who sees others as helpless or sees yourself as a hero. This attitude can be another form of ego. Helping someone is different from treating them as if they cannot do anything without you. A balanced approach is to assist when needed but also encourage them to solve problems on their own when possible.

Community or Volunteer Involvement

Taking part in community programs or volunteer groups can expand your perspective. You see people from different backgrounds and understand various challenges. You also see how your efforts, combined with others', can bring about positive change. Over time, this fosters a sense that the world is bigger than your personal circle.

Listening for Others' Goals
Sometimes, you might only talk about your ambitions—where you want to go, what you want to achieve. By asking, "What are you hoping to do next year?" or "Is there something you have been dreaming about?" you learn about the person's aims. Then you can cheer them on or offer help if it fits. This shift from your goals to theirs nurtures a sense of shared support.

Being There in Tough Times
It is easy to focus on yourself when everything is going well, but looking beyond your own needs becomes vital when someone is having a hard time. If a friend is ill, a family member is grieving, or a coworker is under extreme stress, you can offer small comforts—like cooking a simple meal, sending a thoughtful message, or just sitting and listening. Even if you do not have the perfect words, your presence can make a difference.

Finding Joy in Shared Success
A sign that you are moving away from harmful self-focus is when you feel glad for others' achievements. Maybe a coworker got a promotion you also wanted. While you might feel a bit disappointed for yourself, you can still genuinely congratulate them. Over time, celebrating others' wins becomes more natural, and it enriches your relationships because you show that you care about their victories too.

Respecting Different Approaches
Looking beyond your own needs also means tolerating differences in how people do things. You might be sure your approach is best, but others may have methods that work for them. By respecting these choices, you allow for diversity in solutions. You learn from each other instead of always trying to prove your way is the only way.

Balancing Assertiveness with Care
You can stand up for your rights and share your opinions without neglecting other people's feelings. For instance, in a meeting, you can say, "I want to propose my idea, but I also want to hear what everyone thinks." This signals that

you value both your own voice and the group's input. Over time, people see you as both confident and considerate.

Adjusting Roles in Relationships
In some relationships, you might be used to being the center of attention. Maybe your friend group always follows your plans. Shifting focus might mean encouraging someone else to pick a restaurant or activity. Or if you are always on the receiving end of help, you might try offering help back. Changing these patterns can feel strange at first but leads to healthier, more balanced bonds.

Staying Aware of Self-Focused Urges
Even if you practice caring about others, old habits might pop up. You might catch yourself steering conversations back to you or ignoring another person's needs. This is normal. Just notice it, pause, and gently correct the behavior. Over time, the habit of looking outward becomes more natural.

Examples of Helpful Shifts in Everyday Life

- **At Home:** If you share space, do not leave chores for others because you assume they have more time. Do your share or even help a bit more if someone is having a tough day.
- **At Work:** If a colleague is struggling with a project and you have the know-how, offer a tip or a short demonstration.
- **In Friendships:** Instead of always choosing the activity you love, ask your friend what they would like to do.

These everyday changes show you respect the people around you and care about their comfort.

Listening to Others' Limits
If you ask someone for a favor and they say they are too busy, do not take it as a personal insult. Recognize they might have valid reasons, just as you sometimes do. Accepting their "no" with understanding shows you are aware that other people's time and energy matter, too.

Being Grateful for Support
When you look beyond yourself, you also notice how many people are supporting you in ways big or small. A friend who cheers you on, a coworker who shares knowledge, a neighbor who keeps an eye on your mailbox while you are

away—these are all acts of kindness. Recognize and thank these people. Gratitude reinforces a sense that we all rely on each other.

Not All Help Is Obvious
Sometimes, the greatest help you can give is emotional support, not doing tasks. Listening when someone is sad, or giving a gentle word of encouragement when they feel doubtful, can be priceless. Do not underestimate the power of understanding and kindness in tough moments.

Conclusion
Looking past your own needs does not mean you stop caring for yourself. Instead, it means you widen your vision, seeing yourself as part of a larger group of humans who each have needs, strengths, and struggles. This perspective helps you connect more deeply with friends, family, and even strangers. It also complements other ideas in this book: empathy, setting boundaries, and managing harmful habits.

By noticing what others might need, you move away from self-centered patterns and discover the rewards of sharing, helping, and building together. This approach builds trust and warmth in your relationships, because people sense your genuine concern. It also reduces the pressure you might feel if your whole world centers on being impressive or perfect. In the upcoming chapters, you will continue learning ways to maintain a balanced mind, care for emotional wounds, and pursue lasting positive change. For now, remember that taking a moment to see beyond your personal wants can create a kinder, more supportive world for everyone involved—and that includes you.

Chapter 17: Empathy in Daily Life

Empathy is more than just understanding someone's feelings on a general level. It is also about putting that understanding into practice in simple, everyday situations. When you make empathy a normal part of your routine, you improve not only your own well-being but also the well-being of people around you. This chapter explains how to make empathy a regular habit, from the time you wake up until you go to sleep. By using the ideas here, you can make a real and positive impact on your home, work, or any other place where you connect with others.

Starting the Day with an Empathetic Mindset
Mornings can be rushed or tense, but they also offer an opportunity to set the mood for the rest of the day. If you wake up and immediately feel worried about tasks or problems, empathy might not even cross your mind. One way to shift this is by pausing for a moment to think about the people you will meet or talk to during the day.

- **Simple Morning Reflection:**
    - Ask yourself, "Who might I talk to today? Is there someone who could use a supportive word?"
    - This short mental check prepares you to look beyond your own concerns. You might remember that a coworker was stressed yesterday or that a friend had a medical appointment.

By doing this, you begin the day with an outward view. You stay aware of what others might be feeling, which helps you respond in a kinder way.

Empathy at Home
The place where empathy can be most noticeable is often the place where you feel most at ease—your own home. Family members or roommates see each other's moods up close, and small changes can have large effects.

- **Listening over Breakfast:** If you eat together, ask how each person slept or if they have anything important happening later. Truly listen to their answers.

- **Noticing Stress:** If someone seems tense or quiet, you might gently ask, "Is there anything on your mind?" Without pushing, this shows you care.
- **Showing Gratitude:** Thank family members for simple tasks, like putting away dishes. Even if chores are expected, a brief thank-you can lift the mood.

These small acts might only take seconds, but they set a tone of mutual respect and emotional safety.

Kindness While Commuting
If you travel to school or work, there are chances to show empathy, even in the middle of a crowded bus or on a busy road:

- **On Public Transport:** Offer your seat if you see someone who seems to need it, like an older person or someone carrying a heavy bag.
- **Respecting Personal Space:** Commuting can be stressful. Let people have a bit of room if possible. If someone looks upset, a calm, understanding smile might help them feel less uneasy.
- **Patience in Traffic:** Instead of honking or feeling rage when someone is slow, consider that they might be new to the area or dealing with a car issue. Empathy reminds you not to take delays too personally.

Though these moments are small, they build an inner habit of compassion and reduce negative feelings that might otherwise consume your trip.

Using Empathy in the Workplace or School
Large portions of your day may be spent at work or in class. People in these environments often face pressure—deadlines, tests, group projects, performance reviews. Showing empathy here can reduce tension and improve teamwork:

- **Greet People Warmly:** A genuine "How are you today?" can open conversations. Listen to responses rather than just moving on.
- **Check for Unseen Struggles:** If a coworker or classmate is falling behind, they might have personal problems at home. Before judging them as lazy, try asking if everything is okay. Offer help where reasonable.

- **Give Constructive Feedback, Not Just Criticism:** If you notice an error in a colleague's work, point it out with care. Offer a solution or share a resource that might help them do better next time.

Over time, this thoughtful approach creates a network of people who trust each other and share problems more openly, leading to better problem-solving and less stress.

Showing Empathy to Strangers
You do not need to know someone personally to feel compassion for them. Strangers in stores, on sidewalks, or in online forums are still people with their own feelings:

- **Waiting in Line:** If the line is long, a bit of patience and a friendly nod toward others can ease tension. If someone is in a hurry, you might let them go ahead, especially if they have fewer items or look distressed.
- **Customer Service Workers:** These workers often deal with unhappy or rushed customers. A polite tone and a friendly comment can brighten their day, and it costs you nothing but a moment of kindness.
- **Online Interactions:** If you are on social media or forums, respond with respect even if you disagree. Recognize that the person on the other side is real.

These daily encounters might seem tiny, yet they can build a wider culture of care in your community.

Empathy During Conflicts
Even the most empathetic person will face disagreements or conflicts. In fact, conflict often reveals how much empathy you truly use. During arguments, people can become defensive, thinking only about proving themselves right. Pausing to see the other side's perspective can cool the temperature of the conversation:

- **Reflect the Other Person's Feelings:** Say something like, "I hear you are upset because you think I ignored your request. Is that correct?" This shows you are acknowledging their concerns, not dismissing them.

- **Use a Calm Tone:** Raising your voice or sneering can intensify the problem. A measured, calm tone keeps the focus on the issue at hand, not on personal attacks.
- **Look for Middle Ground:** If possible, suggest a step that could satisfy both sides. Even small agreements can show that you value the other person's needs.

In many cases, empathy in conflict leads to more effective resolutions and less lasting bitterness.

Supporting Friends and Family in Need
You might have people in your life who are facing health problems, job loss, or emotional distress. Here, empathy can go beyond words:

- **Offer Practical Help:** Maybe cook a simple meal, help with errands, or babysit their children. Ask what would ease their stress.
- **Listen Without Quick Fixes:** Sometimes, they only need someone to hear their worries. Offering solutions right away can make them feel rushed. Instead, listen fully and then ask if they want your input.
- **Respect Boundaries:** Some people might not feel ready to share. Let them know you are available when they need you, but do not force them to talk.

Genuine empathy in these moments can help someone feel less alone, reminding them that people care about their situation.

Empathy with Children
If you have children in your life—your own or younger relatives—you can use empathy to guide them:

- **Hearing Their Feelings:** Kids might act out because they do not yet know how to voice emotions. Instead of simply scolding, try asking, "You seem upset. Can you tell me what's bothering you?"
- **Modeling Empathy:** Let them see how you treat others with kindness. Children often copy what they observe.
- **Teaching Them to Notice Others:** Encourage them to ask how a friend is doing or to share a toy with a peer who seems left out. This helps them form caring habits early on.

These actions not only help the child's social development but also reinforce your own understanding of empathy as you see the impact on them.

Self-Awareness for Better Empathy

To maintain empathy each day, you must also stay aware of your own emotional state. If you are exhausted, anxious, or overwhelmed, showing empathy can feel more difficult:

- **Check Your Moods:** At various points in the day, ask yourself, "Am I feeling tense or impatient right now?" If yes, that might be why you are quick to snap or ignore someone.
- **Take Short Breaks:** A moment of quiet or a few deep breaths can reduce stress so you can be more present for others.
- **Set Realistic Goals:** You cannot solve every problem or be there for everyone. Knowing your limits helps you offer help without burning out.

Taking these steps ensures that your empathy remains genuine and not forced.

Teamwork and Group Projects

Whether you are planning a family vacation or collaborating on a work presentation, empathy helps the process go smoothly:

- **Ask for Everyone's Input:** Let each member share ideas. Even if their idea is not used, they feel heard.
- **Watch for Discomfort:** Someone might not speak up if they feel overshadowed. Invite them gently to share their thoughts, or talk to them in private if you notice they never speak in the group.
- **Respect Different Styles:** Some people work better quietly, while others enjoy lively debate. Empathy means giving room for various working methods instead of insisting on only your style.

By ensuring everyone feels included, you build a stronger and more effective team.

Making Space for Others' Stories

Part of daily empathy is making room for stories that are not your own. You might have a coworker from a different country or a friend of another faith background. Being willing to hear their stories fosters empathy:

- **Ask Gently About Their Experiences:** "What was it like growing up where you lived?" or "How does your family do things?"
- **Avoid Quick Judgments:** If their ways differ from yours, keep an open mind and acknowledge that different is not necessarily bad.
- **Offer Your Own Stories Too:** Sharing is a two-way process. Let them learn about you as well, so the bond grows in both directions.

This openness helps you see the world through various viewpoints, deepening your ability to care.

Handling Stressful Situations with Compassion
Life can present challenging moments—illness, financial problems, or other setbacks. Whether they happen to you or to someone you know, empathy can provide a supportive foundation:

- **When You Are the One in Stress:** You might be less patient with others. Recognize this and calmly explain, "I'm under a lot of pressure right now, so if I seem distant, it's not about you."
- **When Someone Else Is in Stress:** Avoid phrases like "Relax" or "It's not a big deal." Instead, say, "I'm sorry you're going through this. Is there a way I can help?"

This approach keeps empathy alive, even in hard times.

Empathy in Personal Decisions
Your personal choices—what you buy, how you spend money, how you treat the environment—can reflect empathy:

- **Thinking About Impacts:** When you consider a purchase, think about whether it supports fair labor or if it harms the environment. Empathy can guide you to make kinder choices.
- **Being Considerate of Neighbors:** If you hold a loud event at your place, inform neighbors in advance or keep noise within reasonable limits. This shows you respect their comfort.
- **Using Resources Wisely:** If you have enough, consider donating items or funds to people who have less. Even small acts can improve someone's life.

These daily decisions quietly strengthen a mindset that sees beyond self-interest.

Handling Negative Reactions

Sometimes, you try to be empathetic, but people respond with anger or they do not want your help. This can feel discouraging:

- **Keep Calm:** Realize their reaction might come from deep stress, mistrust, or previous bad experiences.
- **Do Not Force Help:** If they refuse your support, respect their choice. Let them know you are there if they change their mind.
- **Reflect Later:** Ask yourself if your approach was truly helpful or if it came across as intrusive. You can adjust next time.

Empathy does not guarantee you will always be welcomed with open arms, but it does mean you are offering genuine care.

Balancing Empathy with Personal Boundaries

Showing empathy does not mean sacrificing your own needs at every turn:

- **Recognize Overextension:** If you are tired or overwhelmed, you cannot offer quality help. Sometimes, you must rest or politely say, "I'm sorry, but I can't right now."
- **Suggest Alternative Sources of Help:** If someone's need is beyond what you can handle, you might guide them to professional resources or other supportive networks.
- **Stay Honest:** Pretending you can handle everything might lead to resentment or burnout. Empathy includes honesty about what you can and cannot do.

Maintaining these limits helps your empathy stay strong and consistent instead of becoming a chore.

Reflecting at Day's End

Just like starting your morning with an outward view, ending your day with a small empathy check can reinforce the habit:

- **Ask Yourself:** "Did I show kindness today?" or "Was there a moment I dismissed someone's feelings?"
- **Notice Missed Chances:** If you realize you brushed someone off, think about how you might respond differently next time.
- **Recognize Achievements:** It is fine to quietly appreciate the times you did listen or help, reminding yourself that empathy is an ongoing practice.

This daily reflection helps you refine your approach over time, turning empathy into a natural part of your character.

Teaching Empathy Through Example

If you have any leadership role—parent, mentor, supervisor—you can influence how others learn empathy:

- **Model the Behavior:** When they see you respond calmly to a rude comment, they learn how to handle conflict.
- **Praise Thoughtful Acts:** If you see a student or coworker act kindly, offer a word of appreciation: "That was very considerate. Thank you for helping."
- **Encourage Group Solutions:** In a team, ask people to consider each other's viewpoints before deciding on a plan.

Leading by example is often more effective than giving speeches about empathy.

Adapting Empathy to Different Personalities

You might find empathy easier with people whose feelings mirror your own. But what about those who seem distant, gruff, or have a very different style?

- **Acknowledge Their Style:** Some individuals prefer direct talk and might seem rude if you expect gentle conversation. You can still be empathetic by calmly acknowledging their concerns.
- **Stay Respectful:** Even if they do not offer empathy back, you can maintain a respectful tone. This might soften them over time.
- **Give Them Space:** If someone is very private, they might reject open displays of concern. That is okay; let them know you are available if they ever need to talk.

The key is to meet people where they are, without imposing your own communication style on them.

Diversity of Needs

Every person has unique emotional needs, personalities, and backgrounds. By appreciating this variety, you avoid judging them solely by your own standards. This stance allows empathy to flourish because you recognize that what comforts one person might not comfort another:

- **Ask What Helps Them Feel Supported:** Some people like hugs; others prefer a quiet word of reassurance.
- **Respect Cultural Factors:** In some cultures, it is normal to be very expressive; in others, people may keep emotions more private. Empathy means understanding these differences.

Embracing these variations makes your empathy more accurate and effective.

Carrying Empathy Forward

As you build empathy into your daily life, you will likely see the benefits: calmer interactions, stronger relationships, and a gentler inner state. It is not about being perfect—moments will arise when stress or anger takes over. Yet each time you choose to see and feel for another person, you strengthen a powerful habit.

- **Small Steps Add Up:** A kind word here, a listening ear there, can transform how people relate to you—and how you view yourself.
- **Daily Practice Matters:** Much like exercise, empathy grows with consistent effort.
- **Stay Open to Learning:** Each encounter is a lesson. Reflect on what went well and what could be improved, and apply it in the future.

Through these simple, everyday acts of compassion, you are gradually creating a more peaceful and understanding environment. Empathy moves from an abstract idea to something woven into your entire day. This deepens your ties with others, allows you to manage conflicts more kindly, and helps you feel grounded in a sense of shared humanity.

Chapter 18: Keeping a Balanced Mind

A balanced mind is neither overly positive nor overly negative. It stays steady, handling life's ups and downs with a calm center. People who have struggled with narcissistic traits or strong self-focus might find their thoughts swinging between inflated highs ("I'm the best!") and crushing lows ("I'm terrible!"). This chapter explains ways to keep your thoughts and feelings in a steady zone, so you can respond wisely to challenges and remain open to the needs of others.

Why a Balanced Mind Is Important
A balanced mind does not mean you never feel strong emotions. It means you can experience those emotions without losing control or becoming blinded by them. This balanced approach supports healthy relationships, reduces stress, and helps you make better choices, both for yourself and for those around you.

- **Stability Over Extremes:** Instead of seeing events as perfect or disastrous, you can see them as part of life's natural flow.
- **Less Self-Centered Anxiety:** If you are not always panicked about your status or value, you have more room to think about others.
- **Greater Emotional Resilience:** You bounce back from setbacks more easily because you do not interpret every failure as a total catastrophe.

Understanding Emotional Fluctuations
Most people shift emotionally in response to events—a kind remark can lift your mood, a rude comment can sour it. That is normal. However, when the swings become too intense, they can interfere with daily life. You might snap at others for small reasons or feel worthless if a tiny thing goes wrong.

- **Examples of Emotional Swings:**
    1. Feeling extremely proud one moment, then feeling deep shame the next because someone offered mild criticism.
    2. Believing you have everything under control, then feeling panicked over a minor delay.

Recognizing these patterns is the first step toward finding balance. A balanced mind acknowledges the problem without letting it define your entire worth.

Practicing Mindful Breathing
Breathing exercises remain one of the simplest and most effective methods for regaining mental balance:

- **Basic Method:**
    1. Inhale slowly through your nose for a count of four.
    2. Hold for one second.
    3. Exhale gently through your mouth for a count of four.

Repeat a few times, paying attention to each breath. This pattern can reduce heart rate and calm racing thoughts. By focusing on your breath, you anchor yourself in the present instead of being swept away by worries or anger.

Grounding Techniques
When emotions spin out of control, grounding exercises help you reconnect with your immediate surroundings:

- **Name Five Things:** Look around and quietly name five objects you see: "A clock, a lamp, a book, a window, a chair."
- **Pay Attention to Senses:** Notice one thing you can smell, one thing you can taste, or how your feet feel on the floor.
- **Touch or Texture:** Hold an object—a smooth rock or a soft cloth—and focus on its texture, weight, and temperature.

These tricks pull your mind back from worrying or looping thoughts, promoting a sense of calm.

Balancing Inner Voice
Your internal thoughts can tilt your mood heavily. If they are harsh—"You always fail," "Nobody likes you"—you might believe these untrue statements. Balancing your mind requires challenging these thoughts:

- **Identify Negative Self-Talk:** Notice when you say things to yourself that you would never say to a friend.
- **Counter with Reason:** Ask, "Is it true I always fail? Or have I succeeded sometimes?"
- **Use Calmer Language:** Replace "I can't handle anything" with "This is tough, but I have handled similar problems before."

Shifting your inner voice from extreme put-downs to more measured statements helps keep your emotional levels steady.

Avoiding Over-Interpretation
People with unstable thinking might read too much into small events—an unreturned text becomes a sign that a friend hates them; a coworker's neutral tone becomes proof they look down on you. This over-interpretation fuels anxiety and unneeded conflict:

- **Ask for Clarity:** If unsure, politely ask the person, "Did you mean anything special by that?" Often, they did not.
- **Use More Plausible Explanations:** Maybe your friend is busy, or the coworker is tired. Not everything is about you.
- **Wait Before Reacting:** Give a little time instead of instantly jumping to conclusions.

By challenging these assumptions, you maintain a calmer mind and avoid unnecessary drama.

Keeping a Realistic Perspective
A balanced mind also sees personal successes and failures in perspective. If you do well on a task, you can feel proud without believing you are perfect. If you mess up, you can feel disappointed but remind yourself that one error does not define you.

- **Healthy Response to Success:** "I did a good job, and I'm glad. I can keep building on this."
- **Healthy Response to Failure:** "I learned something here. I can adjust and try again."

This middle-ground perspective prevents inflated highs and crushing lows, stabilizing your sense of self-worth.

Setting Reasonable Goals
Unrealistic goals can lead to stress and frustration, causing large mood swings when you inevitably fall short. A balanced mind approach is to set goals that push you a little but remain doable:

- **Small Steps:** Instead of aiming to master a skill in a week, break it into daily or weekly improvements.

- **Update Goals as Needed:** If you find the goal too easy or too hard, adjust it instead of giving up or feeling like a failure.

Limiting Excessive Self-Comparison

Comparing yourself to others—especially those on social media who appear always happy—can erode balance. You might see a curated image of perfection and feel terrible about your own normal ups and downs. A balanced approach is to recognize that social media often highlights the best moments, not the full reality:

- **Focus on Personal Growth:** Track your own progress over time rather than measuring yourself against others.
- **Take Breaks from Social Media:** If you notice your mood sinking after seeing others' posts, give yourself a rest from scrolling.
- **Admire Without Envy:** It is fine to be inspired by someone's achievements, but remember they also have struggles you may not see.

Practicing Self-Care

Maintaining a balanced mind requires taking care of your body and mental state:

- **Regular Sleep:** Lack of proper rest can increase irritability and unsteady emotions. Aim for a consistent sleep schedule.
- **Healthy Eating:** Sugary, processed foods can cause energy spikes and crashes. A balanced diet helps stabilize mood.
- **Physical Activity:** Even light exercise, like walking, can lift your mood and reduce stress.
- **Relaxation or Hobbies:** Spend some time on activities that calm you or give you gentle pleasure, such as reading or drawing.

These simple habits keep your baseline mood steadier, making it easier to respond calmly when stress appears.

Planning for Stressful Events

Certain moments—like major deadlines, family gatherings, or public speaking—can trigger anxiety or mood swings. Instead of waiting for the worst to happen, prepare in advance:

- **Visualize Calmly Handling It:** Imagine yourself dealing with the situation step by step, staying composed.

- **Outline Support:** If you have a presentation, practice with a friend. If a family event is tense, plan how you might leave early if needed.
- **Use Soothing Tools:** Keep a stress ball, comforting music, or a short relaxation technique ready.

By taking these steps, you give yourself the best chance to remain steady rather than being caught off guard.

Managing Anger and Resentment
Anger often knocks people off balance. One minor trigger can unleash a strong reaction. Recognizing early signs—such as clenched fists or a racing heart—lets you pause:

- **Take a Time-Out:** If you can, step away from the situation for a moment to breathe.
- **Use a Calm-Down Phrase:** Quietly tell yourself, "I can handle this" or "Breathe and think first."
- **Reframe the Situation:** Instead of labeling someone as evil or rude, consider if they might be stressed or unaware of how they affect you.

This approach prevents anger from making you say or do things you regret later.

Accepting Change and Uncertainty
Life is full of changes—jobs can shift, friendships evolve, health can vary. A balanced mind does not cling too tightly to things staying exactly as they are:

- **See Change as Natural:** Remind yourself that everyone experiences changes, not just you.
- **Focus on What You Can Control:** You cannot stop every change, but you can control your response.
- **Explore Solutions:** If a change is negative, look for constructive ways to adapt rather than sitting in frustration.

By staying flexible, you reduce the shock when life takes an unexpected turn, and your mood stays steadier.

Healthy Ways to Process Sadness
Sadness is a normal emotion, sometimes triggered by loss or disappointment. Trying to avoid it entirely can backfire, causing deeper mood swings later:

- **Name the Feeling:** Simply saying, "I am sad right now," can be a relief.
- **Write About It:** Journaling can help you understand why you feel this way.
- **Allow Gentle Comfort:** Talk to a trusted friend or do something soothing, like sipping tea and listening to calming music.
- **Avoid Hiding It:** Pretending you are not sad can lead to bottled-up feelings that emerge as anger or despair.

Processing sadness in a healthy manner keeps it from dominating your mind.

Combining Structure with Flexibility

A routine can help keep your emotions steady. Going to bed at a similar time, keeping a regular mealtime, and scheduling time for tasks can reduce chaos. At the same time, being too rigid can cause stress if something disrupts your plan. Aim for a middle ground:

- **Have a General Schedule:** Know when you will do chores, rest, and social activities.
- **Allow Wiggle Room:** If your friend needs help unexpectedly, you can adjust without feeling your entire day is ruined.
- **Keep Priorities Clear:** If your main goal is to stay balanced, you will not let small disruptions create panic.

Staying Away from Extremes in Speech

Using words like "always" or "never" can feed extreme thinking, like "They never help me," or "I always mess up." This type of language amplifies negativity. Try to be more specific:

- **Instead of:** "I always fail at everything."
- **Use:** "I failed at this one attempt, but I have had successes before."

This precise language reduces all-or-nothing thoughts, making your mind calmer and more measured.

Learning to Let Go of Control

If you have a habit of wanting everything to go your way, you may become upset whenever events differ from your plan. A balanced mind recognizes that some factors are beyond your control. Accepting this can prevent large emotional swings:

- **Focus on Your Choices:** You can control how you talk, how you prepare, and how you respond.
- **Release the Rest:** You cannot control weather, traffic, or another person's feelings. Trying to do so often leads to frustration.
- **Practice Calm Acceptance:** When something unexpected happens, remind yourself you can adapt instead of seeing it as a personal failure.

Seeking Support When Needed
Trying to maintain a balanced mind alone can be challenging if you have long-term stress, anxiety, or unresolved issues. There is no shame in asking for help:

- **Friends or Family:** Sometimes, talking it out can help you see solutions or simply feel less burdened.
- **Counselors or Therapists:** They have training in helping people find steadiness and cope with strong emotions.
- **Support Groups:** Sharing experiences with others who face similar challenges can provide relief and practical tips.

This support system can keep you from sliding into extreme states when life becomes overwhelming.

Resisting Quick Fixes
In seeking balance, some people turn to short-term solutions that can cause harm, such as substance abuse or other harmful behaviors. These might numb emotions briefly but usually create bigger problems later. True balance comes from steady habits and honest self-reflection, not from escaping feelings through unwise actions.

Small Daily Practices for Balance
Integrating easy routines can help your mind stay in a comfortable zone:

- **Morning Grounding:** Upon waking, spend one minute noticing your breath and stretching gently.
- **Midday Check-In:** At lunch, pause to observe how you feel. Are you tense, worried, or relaxed? Identify the emotion without judgment.
- **Evening Reflection:** Before sleep, recall one thing that was difficult and one thing that went well. This balanced view stops you from dwelling only on troubles.

These small steps, done consistently, build mental steadiness over time.

Balancing Empathy and Self-Protection

As you practice empathy, you may feel overwhelmed by others' sadness or anger. A balanced mind manages empathy in a healthy way:

- **Recognize Your Limits:** If listening to someone's problems is draining you too much, you can politely pause or suggest a different time.
- **Use Short Breaks:** After an intense talk, step away for a few deep breaths or a quick walk.
- **Avoid Over-Identifying:** Being empathetic does not mean taking on their emotions as your own. Offer understanding while keeping your own emotional footing.

Learning from Mistakes Without Self-Punishment

Mistakes and missteps are natural. If you respond by beating yourself up, you risk tipping into negative extremes. A balanced response might be:

- **Admit the Mistake Calmly:** "Yes, I did that incorrectly."
- **Correct It If Possible:** Offer to fix the error or apologize if needed.
- **Plan for Next Time:** Think about a strategy to avoid the same mistake. Then let it go.

This method of facing errors supports steady self-esteem.

Regular Physical Movement

A quick stretch, a short walk, or dancing to your favorite music can dispel built-up tension in your body. Tension often fuels mental unsteadiness. Even a few minutes of movement each hour can keep your energy balanced.

Balancing the Desire for Approval

Everyone enjoys praise, but relying too heavily on it can cause big mood swings. If you get praise, you feel ecstatic; if you do not, you feel ignored or worthless. Keep this in check by reminding yourself that your value is not decided by others' compliments. Accept praise graciously, but do not let it be your sole source of self-worth.

Scheduling Digital Downtime

Constant notifications, emails, and social media updates can overstimulate your mind. If you set times of the day to put away your phone or shut off notifications, you create space for calm:

- **No-Phone Meals:** Keep your device away while eating to enjoy your food and any company you have.
- **Bedtime Boundaries:** Avoid looking at screens an hour before sleep if you can.
- **Short Breaks After Work or School:** Give yourself 15–30 minutes away from screens before moving on to other tasks.

This helps prevent mental overload and fosters a more peaceful mood.

Recognizing Emotional Drainers
Some activities or people might repeatedly leave you feeling unbalanced. This does not mean you must abandon them entirely, but awareness helps you manage interactions better:

- **If Certain Topics Trigger You:** Limit how long you talk about them, or prepare coping strategies beforehand.
- **If a Relationship Is Constantly Negative:** Consider whether you can set boundaries or seek counseling for that dynamic.
- **If an Activity Worsens Your Mood:** Reflect on whether it is essential. If not, reduce it or change how you approach it.

Speaking Kindly, Even to Yourself
The way you talk to yourself or about yourself affects your mental balance. Use a tone that is fair and kind, the same way you would want a friend to speak to you:

- **Avoid Mean Labels:** Replace "I'm an idiot" with "I made an error."
- **Use Gentle Encouragement:** "I'm learning each day. I can improve step by step."
- **Practice Compassion:** Remind yourself that everyone is imperfect, and that is okay.

Welcoming Calmness as Strength
In some cultures, being loud and aggressive is seen as strong, while calmness might be viewed as weak. A balanced mind recognizes that calmness is actually a powerful state—one where you can think clearly, avoid rash decisions, and treat others with respect.

Sharing Your Tips with Others
Once you find ways that help you stay balanced, share them with friends or family if they seem open. Simple reminders like "Have you tried pausing to breathe?" can help someone else who is overwhelmed. Teaching or suggesting these tools also reinforces your own practice, because it keeps them fresh in your mind.

Conclusion
Keeping a balanced mind is a daily practice that brings peace and improves how you relate to the world. It guards against extreme highs and lows, letting you see events and people more clearly. While life will still bring stress and sadness, a steady mental state helps you face these challenges without losing your center.

By using mindful breathing, grounding techniques, self-care, and realistic thoughts, you create a more stable environment inside yourself. This steadiness allows you to respond to others with empathy, handle criticism without falling apart, and accept that some moments will be difficult while others will be easier. Over time, your balanced mind can become a trustworthy ally, guiding you toward wiser choices and kinder interactions every day.

As you move forward in your personal changes, remember that balance is not about never feeling strong emotion. It is about managing those emotions in a way that respects both your own needs and the needs of the people around you. That approach fits well with the earlier steps discussed—practicing empathy, setting boundaries, looking beyond your own interests—and it paves the way for the final chapters, where we will address healing emotional wounds and making lasting, positive adjustments in your life.

Chapter 19: Mending Emotional Wounds

Emotional wounds happen when our feelings are deeply hurt or when we experience a kind of loss that leaves us feeling incomplete, broken, or unable to move forward. These wounds can come from many places: conflicts in childhood, broken trust in relationships, painful experiences of being ignored or rejected, or even a single moment of intense shock. When these wounds stay untreated, they may shape our view of ourselves and the world. They can make us hide from connections, distrust others, or stay locked in harmful patterns of self-focus.

However, mending emotional wounds is possible. It involves honesty about what happened, recognizing the lingering pain, and choosing to heal. This chapter explores practical steps you can use to address old hurts and build healthier emotional habits. By facing emotional wounds, you create space to feel calmer and to give and receive care more freely.

Recognizing Hidden Wounds
Emotional wounds do not always show up as obvious sadness or anger. Sometimes, they stay hidden behind behaviors such as:

- **Avoiding Close Relationships:** You might keep people at a distance to avoid being hurt again.
- **Seeking Constant Approval:** Perhaps you feel unworthy deep down and try to fill the gap by chasing praise.
- **Feeling Overly Defensive:** Even mild comments can feel like attacks if your past hurt is unaddressed.
- **Shame or Guilt:** You might blame yourself for what happened, thinking you deserved the pain.

By noticing these patterns, you can start seeing if they link to unhealed emotional wounds. Awareness is often the first sign that there is something deeper needing care.

Why Healing Matters
When emotional injuries remain unresolved, they can affect everyday life. You may:

- **Struggle to Trust People:** The fear of being hurt again can make you suspicious or guarded.
- **Carry Resentment or Anger:** Old hurts can build bitterness toward certain people or situations, leading to overreactions in the present.
- **Use Harmful Coping Methods:** Some try to numb the hurt through behaviors that damage health or relationships.
- **Miss Out on Calmness and Joy:** The wound can be like a weight, dragging down your sense of peace.

Choosing to mend these hurts allows you to move forward without bringing the old pain into every new situation. It frees you to form healthier connections and develop a balanced sense of self.

Facing the Root Cause
Healing starts by understanding what caused the hurt and why it still lingers. For some, the wound may trace back to childhood experiences, like a parent who did not show support. For others, it could stem from a betrayal in a romantic relationship, a deep friendship rift, or bullying at school. To see the root cause:

- **Reflect Honestly:** Ask, "Which events in my past still make me feel pain or anger when I recall them?"
- **Write It Down:** Journaling can help you explore memories and feelings you might have pushed aside.
- **Notice Emotional Triggers:** If you react strongly to certain situations, ask yourself if it connects to a past hurt.

Accepting the Feelings
Emotional wounds can bring sadness, anger, or shame. Sometimes, you might feel embarrassed or weak for having these feelings. But to heal, you have to accept that these emotions are real and valid. Denying them only lets them grow in the background.

- **Name Your Emotions:** Clearly identify if you feel anger, fear, grief, or another emotion.
- **Allow Yourself to Feel It:** Instead of pushing it away, say, "It's okay to feel hurt." This does not mean you wallow in sadness forever; it is a step in recognizing the wound.

- **Avoid Self-Judgment:** Telling yourself, "I should be over this," can make healing harder. Grief and pain vary from person to person.

Seeking Safe Outlets

Healing rarely happens in a vacuum. It often requires a safe way to release the emotions tied to past injuries:

- **Talk to a Trusted Friend or Counselor:** Speaking your pain out loud can lessen its hold. A counselor can guide you in processing the event and your reactions.
- **Write Letters You Do Not Send:** If someone hurt you and you never got closure, drafting a letter can free some of the built-up anger or sadness. You do not have to mail it.
- **Creative Expression:** Drawing, painting, playing music, or creating something can provide a nonverbal channel for releasing inner burdens.

Having these safe outlets ensures you are not alone with your pain, which helps prevent destructive coping methods.

Deciding If Confrontation Helps

Sometimes, a person may feel the need to speak with the one who caused the hurt. This can bring closure or understanding, but it must be approached carefully:

- **Check If It Is Safe:** If the other person is aggressive or not likely to respond well, direct confrontation might cause more harm.
- **Have Clear Goals:** Know what you want from the meeting—a sincere apology, an explanation, or simply expressing your feelings.
- **Stay Calm and Respectful:** If you become confrontational or insulting, it might lead to a bigger conflict.

However, even if direct contact is not possible or wise, you can still heal. Sometimes, writing a letter you never send is enough to release built-up emotions.

Understanding Forgiveness

Forgiveness does not mean agreeing that the harm was okay, nor does it mean allowing the same harm to happen again. Instead, forgiveness is about freeing yourself from carrying around anger or the wish for revenge:

- **Choosing to Let Go of Resentment:** By releasing the hold that past wrongdoing has on your heart, you free up emotional energy for better things.
- **Setting Healthier Boundaries If Needed:** You can forgive someone yet decide to limit or end the relationship if they are harmful.
- **Allowing Room for Growth:** Sometimes, forgiveness opens a path for the other person to make amends, but you are not responsible for fixing them.

Forgiveness is an act of self-care. It stops the past from dominating the present, letting you move forward without bitterness dragging you down.

Overcoming Shame

Some emotional wounds revolve around shame: the sense that you are flawed or unworthy. Shame can be tied to events you blame yourself for or times you felt humiliated. Moving past shame involves:

- **Admitting That You Are Not Defined by One Event:** A single mistake or hurtful experience does not sum up your entire worth.
- **Seeing External Factors:** Maybe you were put in a bad situation that was not your fault. Understanding this can loosen shame's grip.
- **Speaking Kindly to Yourself:** Notice negative self-talk, like "I'm bad," and replace it with, "I made a mistake" or "I was treated unfairly, but I can heal."

By shifting how you see yourself, you peel away layers of shame that keep you stuck in old wounds.

Mending Trust

After betrayal, it can be hard to trust again. You might fear that letting anyone close will only bring more pain. Mending trust requires a gradual approach:

- **Trust in Small Steps:** Open up to someone you find relatively safe. Share a bit about yourself and see if they respect your feelings.
- **Observe Reliability:** If someone shows consistent kindness over time, let that evidence speak rather than your old wounds.

- **Set Clear Boundaries:** Healthy boundaries let you feel safe while you practice trust. If you notice red flags, you can step back.

Mending trust does not happen instantly. However, each positive interaction can weaken the hold of past betrayals, allowing you to see that not everyone is out to hurt you.

Managing Triggers

A trigger is something—like a sight, sound, or situation—that reminds you of the wound. It can stir up old hurt or fear. Learning to manage triggers helps you live more freely:

- **Identify Possible Triggers:** Think about situations that cause sudden distress. Is it a certain song, location, or phrase?
- **Plan Coping Methods:** If you must face a trigger, have a plan—like a friend to call or a calming routine.
- **Practice Grounding Exercises:** Use breathing or focusing on your surroundings to stay in the present moment when a trigger appears.

Over time, triggers might fade in power, especially as you work on healing the core wound.

Seeking Professional Support

Some emotional wounds are deep and complex. They may connect to abuse, traumatic events, or long-term neglect. In these cases, professional therapy can be a major help:

- **Types of Therapy:** Different styles exist, such as talk therapy, cognitive-behavioral techniques, or trauma-focused methods. A trained therapist can choose an approach that fits your needs.
- **Guidance in Processing Emotions:** A counselor can give you safe space to explore painful memories and learn practical tools for coping.
- **Support Without Judgment:** Therapists are there to help you heal, not to shame you.

Even if you have mild emotional wounds, therapy can accelerate healing and prevent lingering issues from turning into bigger hurdles.

Healthy Outlets for Pain

Besides professional help, consider everyday ways to express and release emotional burdens:

- **Physical Activities:** Exercise, yoga, or a nature walk can lower stress and calm the mind.
- **Art or Writing:** Channels like painting, sketching, writing poetry, or playing music can transform pain into creation, giving you a sense of relief.
- **Relaxation Methods:** Techniques like meditation or gentle stretches before bed can soothe anxious thoughts.

These outlets remind you that you have choices in handling emotional discomfort. Instead of letting it fester, you can shape it into something manageable.

Rebuilding Self-Worth

Emotional wounds often strike at the core of how we see ourselves. They may convince us we are helpless or not good enough. Rebuilding self-worth involves steady effort:

- **Listing Strengths:** Note your positive traits, like patience, humor, creativity, or loyalty. Look back at times you showed these qualities.
- **Replacing Negative Thoughts:** If your mind says, "I can't do anything right," respond with a calm correction: "I do many things well, even if I am still learning in some areas."
- **Allowing Compliments:** If people praise you, accept it instead of shrugging it off. Let it sink in that others see good in you.

As self-worth grows, past wounds lose some of their power to define you. You realize you have value no matter what happened.

Learning to Trust Yourself

Sometimes, emotional wounds result in doubting your own instincts. You might think you made poor choices, so you no longer trust your decisions:

- **Review Good Choices You Have Made:** Remember times you handled a problem well or stood up for yourself.

- **Start with Small Decisions:** Choose small daily things—like which new meal to cook or a simple place to visit—and trust your own choice. Gradually, move to bigger decisions.
- **Acknowledge Mistakes as Part of Growth:** Everyone errs. One or two missteps do not mean your instincts are always wrong.

Trusting yourself again can reduce the fear of repeating past hurts, because you believe you can handle or avoid them better now.

Giving Yourself Time to Heal
Mending emotional wounds does not happen overnight. Deep hurts can take months or even years to fully mend, and that is okay. Rushing the process or demanding quick fixes can lead to frustration:

- **Be Patient with Setbacks:** Some days, you might feel strong and hopeful; other days, old memories might resurface. This back-and-forth is normal.
- **Measure Progress Gently:** Instead of expecting total healing in a short span, notice smaller steps—like being able to talk about the event without feeling overwhelmed.
- **Keep Support Close:** Friends, family, or a counselor can remind you that healing is a process.

Accepting the natural flow of healing helps you stay motivated, even when progress is not constant.

Understanding When an Apology Might Not Come
Part of healing is facing the fact that the person who hurt you may never apologize or even realize they did harm. This can be tough because we often yearn for them to admit they were wrong. However:

- **Healing Is Your Own Step:** You do not need their confession to move forward.
- **You Can Let Go Without Their Input:** By acknowledging what they did and choosing to release resentment, you claim your own power to heal.
- **Self-Validation:** You can validate your pain. You do not need them to agree it was serious.

Recognizing that closure does not depend on someone else's actions can bring relief and more control over your own emotions.

Avoiding Repeated Patterns

Emotional wounds sometimes make us repeat certain roles—like always choosing friends or partners who treat us poorly or falling into similar conflicts again and again. Breaking these patterns means:

- **Spotting Red Flags Early:** If someone's behavior reminds you of a past harmful relationship, step back to see if it is truly a repeat or just a minor similarity.
- **Setting Boundaries:** Make it clear what you will not tolerate. If they cross that line, consider leaving the situation.
- **Trying Different Responses:** If you always responded with anger in the past, try a calm conversation or a break to think before talking.

Changing your response can shift the outcome. You do not have to relive old hurts in new packages.

Finding Meaning in the Pain

Some people find that acknowledging the lessons they learned from a painful event can help them heal. This does not mean the event was good, but it can mean you grow stronger or wiser:

- **Recognizing a New Strength:** Maybe you discovered you are more resilient than you thought.
- **Developing Empathy for Others:** Feeling deep hurt might deepen your compassion for people who are also suffering.
- **Realizing Your Values:** A betrayal might show you how important honesty or loyalty is to you.

This mindset does not erase the wound, but it can remind you that pain can lead to growth if you allow it.

Helping Others Heal

As you work on your own wounds, you might notice others around you going through similar struggles. Supporting them can also reinforce your own healing:

- **Offering a Listening Ear:** You do not need to be an expert, but letting them talk safely can be a huge comfort.
- **Sharing Tools That Helped You:** If a certain relaxation method, journaling style, or approach to setting boundaries worked for you, mention it.

- **Encouraging Professional Help:** If their wounds are deep, suggest they consider speaking to a counselor.

Being there for someone else can remind you that healing is possible and that everyone deserves understanding and support.

Continuing Self-Care
Once you feel the initial pain softening, do not forget the ongoing care that keeps you emotionally healthy:

- **Stay Attentive to Your Feelings:** If you feel old hurt rising again, take time to handle it instead of ignoring it.
- **Maintain Healthy Boundaries:** Keep your relationships respectful. Speak up if someone's words or actions bring back painful memories.

By continuing to nurture yourself, you ensure that old wounds do not regain their power.

Reaching a Place of Strength
Emotional wounds can leave scars, but scars are not the same as ongoing pain. Over time, the wound can become a mark of something you survived. You might even find that you have more empathy or a greater sense of purpose from having navigated through your hurt.

- **Newfound Courage:** Realizing you faced your pain can boost your confidence.
- **Openness to Connection:** Once fear of being hurt lessens, you can form healthier and deeper bonds with people.
- **Freer Emotional Life:** You no longer have to keep strong walls or distractions to avoid pain. You can live more honestly and calmly.

Mending Wounds and Self-Focus
When emotional wounds remain, a person might become too focused on protecting themselves or proving themselves to others. Healing removes the fear or shame that drives that focus. You can then look outward with more interest in how others feel, because you are not constantly shielding your own hurt or trying to fill a gap. This shift makes empathy and kindness more natural.

Examples of Real Change
Suppose you once felt deeply rejected by a close friend who suddenly ended the

friendship. You might have developed a habit of pulling away from new friends to avoid more rejection. As you heal:

- You acknowledge that the old friend's choice does not mean everyone will leave.
- You forgive them or yourself for that past hurt.
- You slowly open up to new friendships, noticing that some people genuinely care.

Over time, you find you can form trusting bonds again. The old wound no longer controls your present or future relationships.

Combining Healing with Other Parts of Growth

This book has covered empathy, reducing harmful self-focus, setting boundaries, and more. Healing emotional wounds weaves in with all these topics:

- **Empathy:** As you heal, you become more emotionally present, able to sense others' feelings without letting your own pain distort things.
- **Boundaries:** Healing helps you set healthy limits because you better understand your emotional needs.
- **Balanced Mind:** Letting go of old pain frees you from many triggers, making it easier to maintain a calm inner state.

Each step supports the others, leading to a more stable and caring way of living.

Honoring Your Emotional Journey

It is important to remember that healing is personal. One person might find closure quickly, while another may need more time. You might revisit certain wounds if new events remind you of them. That is natural, not a sign of failure.

- **Respect Your Own Pace:** No one can force you to heal faster than feels right for you.
- **Celebrate (Avoiding the forbidden word—Use "acknowledge") Achievements:** When you notice you are less triggered by past events or more open in relationships, quietly acknowledge that progress.
- **Stay Open to the Future:** Healing can reveal new directions for your life, as you are no longer tied to old fears.

Growth Beyond the Wound

Sometimes, in mending an emotional wound, people discover a stronger sense of self. They might find new talents or passions after releasing old baggage. They might become a source of support for others facing similar hurts. Healing does not mean forgetting or denying what happened; it means letting the past shape you in a constructive, wiser way.

Encouraging a Wider Healing Culture

When you share your honest experiences of healing with friends or relatives, you create an environment where others feel safer to address their own emotional wounds. By being open to talking about past hurts in a careful, respectful way, you can help normalize the process of growth and self-awareness. This not only helps you but can also encourage kindness within your social circles.

Maintaining Perspective

Even after significant progress, life can throw new difficulties your way—fresh losses, betrayals, or disappointments. Having healed old wounds does not mean you will never be hurt again. Instead, it means you have learned how to face pain more wisely. You can remind yourself that you have the tools to address new challenges without letting them become permanent scars.

Supporting Someone Else's Healing

If you meet someone who is obviously wounded emotionally, remember what helped you:

- **Listening Over Advising:** Let them express their feelings instead of jumping in with immediate fixes.
- **Respecting Their Timing:** Healing might go more slowly or quickly for them than it did for you. That is normal.
- **Avoiding Judgment:** If they struggle with trust or keep quiet, be patient. Emotional wounds often make people cautious.

By showing compassion, you reinforce your own healing path and help build a supportive community.

Conclusion

Mending emotional wounds is an ongoing process that invites you to be honest, patient, and kind toward yourself. It often requires a look into painful memories, but it also frees you from carrying old burdens that limit your connections and your peace of mind. Through recognizing the hurt, releasing toxic shame or anger, and practicing forgiveness (for yourself or for others), you reclaim parts of yourself that were stuck in the past.

Each step in healing ties in with the other skills in this book—empathy, balanced thinking, healthy boundaries, and self-awareness. Together, they offer a path that moves you out of harmful self-focus and into a healthier, more caring understanding of who you are. In the final chapter, we will look at how to keep these positive changes for the long run. Emotional healing opens the door, and consistent self-reflection and kindness keep you on the path toward lasting growth and calmness.

Chapter 20: Long-Term Positive Change

Having learned about harmful self-focus, empathy, boundaries, inner calm, and ways to heal emotional wounds, the final step is integrating everything into a long-term pattern. Making changes that stick can be challenging, especially when old habits feel familiar. But with steady commitment and practical strategies, you can shape a life that honors both your own well-being and the well-being of those around you. This chapter lays out how to sustain positive changes over time, navigate setbacks, and keep your sense of peace and empathy strong.

Understanding Lasting Change

Short-term changes—like being kinder for a few days—can fade if you return to old habits once the initial motivation passes. Lasting change means building new patterns that continue through everyday stress and temptations. This involves:

- **Deep Personal Commitment:** You choose these changes not just because of a passing idea but because you truly see their value.
- **Practical Routines:** Integrating new behaviors into daily life so they become second nature.
- **Openness to Ongoing Learning:** Realizing you will keep adapting as you discover more about yourself.

Reviewing What You Learned

Over the course of this book, you explored:

- **Spotting Problem Behaviors:** Recognizing signs of excessive self-focus, from always needing attention to dismissing others' needs.
- **Developing Empathy:** Learning how to care about someone else's feelings in real, daily ways.
- **Building Inner Peace:** Practicing breathing, mindfulness, and balanced thinking to handle stress without harming yourself or others.
- **Setting Boundaries:** Respecting your own limits and the limits of others so that everyone's needs are considered.

- **Healing Emotional Wounds:** Addressing past hurts so they no longer define your present.

Think of these areas like pieces of a puzzle. They fit together to form a whole approach to living more kindly and steadily.

Setting Realistic Goals

Long-term positive change is supported by setting specific, reachable goals. Vague aims like "I want to be nicer" can fade because there is no clear way to see progress. Instead:

- **Pick Clear Targets:** For example, "I will listen for at least three minutes before giving my own view in a conversation."
- **Measure Progress:** You might note times you resisted interrupting or times you used mindful breathing instead of snapping at someone.

Keeping a Personal Journal

Writing a few lines each day can help you track your thoughts and behaviors. You can include:

- **Actions You Are Proud Of:** Times you showed empathy or held firm to healthy boundaries.
- **Moments You Struggled:** Where did you slip back into old patterns? Why did it happen?
- **Ideas for Improvement:** What can you do differently next time to handle a similar challenge?

This regular reflection cements your growth and highlights areas still needing attention.

Creating Supportive Surroundings

Your environment can either push you toward change or pull you back. Look around and see what could help your new mindset:

- **Encourage Positive Influences:** Spend more time with friends or family who respect you and encourage thoughtful behavior.
- **Limit Negative Triggers:** If certain people, places, or online spaces feed self-centered thinking or conflict, reduce your involvement or set boundaries.

- **Display Reminders:** Some people put inspiring quotes on their walls or phone backgrounds. Choose phrases that keep you focused on empathy and calm.

Making your surroundings align with your goals makes it easier to keep going when you feel tired or stressed.

Sharing Goals with Trusted People
Telling a friend or loved one about the changes you want to sustain can boost accountability. It feels more real when someone else knows your intentions:

- **Check-Ins:** Ask if they can gently ask you how your empathy practice or boundary-setting is going.
- **Mutual Growth:** Maybe they have goals too, and you can support each other.
- **Honest Feedback:** If you start slipping into self-centered habits, someone who cares might remind you of your commitment.

These social support structures help you stick to your new patterns instead of drifting back to old ways unnoticed.

Learning from Setbacks
Even with the best intentions, you might have days or weeks when you revert to unhealthy behaviors. This is normal. Lasting change does not mean never failing. It means using failures as lessons:

- **Identify the Trigger:** Did stress at work or lack of sleep make you more likely to snap at someone?
- **Plan a Better Response:** Next time that stress appears, what specific action can you try instead? Maybe a short walk, a conversation with a friend, or mindful breathing.
- **Avoid Guilt Spirals:** Feeling guilty for slipping can push you back into old patterns. Instead, accept that you slipped, learn from it, and move on.

Balancing Confidence and Humility
As you see yourself growing, you might be tempted to think you have arrived at the ultimate state or to become proud that you are "better" than others. True growth includes:

- **Confidence in Progress:** Acknowledge that you have made real changes. Let this encourage you to keep going.
- **Humility in Ongoing Learning:** Recognize that you do not know everything and can still grow. Other people may have wisdom to share as well.

This mix ensures you stay open to feedback and remain willing to adapt further.

Checking Your Motivations

Sometimes, it helps to remind yourself why you started this path in the first place:

- **Reducing Harmful Self-Focus:** You realized it was isolating you or causing problems in relationships.
- **Developing Empathy:** You wanted deeper connections and to be kinder.
- **Seeking Inner Peace:** You were tired of emotional roller coasters and craved stability.

Reconnecting with these core motivations can refresh your dedication when the effort feels tiring. Remind yourself that these changes do not just benefit others; they also free you from the weight of living in a constant self-focused cycle.

Adjusting Boundaries over Time

The boundaries you set might need revisiting as your relationships or circumstances evolve:

- **When a Relationship Improves:** You might become more open and willing to share deeper parts of yourself.
- **If New Conflicts Arise:** You might need clearer boundaries if you discover fresh sources of stress.
- **Personal Growth:** As you grow in empathy and self-worth, you might no longer need extremely rigid limits to feel safe.

Staying flexible with boundaries helps you maintain a healthy balance that supports both your own well-being and that of others.

Continuing Empathy Exercises

Empathy is not a one-time lesson; it is a skill that can strengthen with daily practice:

- **Listen Fully Every Day:** Aim to truly listen to at least one person without interrupting or rushing.
- **Ask About Feelings:** When someone shares news—good or bad—ask how they feel about it. This shows genuine care.
- **Observe Body Language:** Notice if a friend or coworker's posture or facial expression shows stress or concern. Offer a supportive word if appropriate.

These ongoing mini-habits keep empathy alive in your routine, even when life gets busy.

Blending Inner Peace with Social Interactions
Maintaining your calm while interacting with others is crucial. The steadier you are inside, the less likely you will revert to self-centered or defensive habits:

- **Pause Before Speaking:** A simple moment to breathe can stop a heated outburst.
- **Stay Mindful in Conversations:** Pay attention to the other person's words, tone, and emotion. Focus on understanding them rather than thinking ahead to what you will say next.
- **Ground Yourself in Stressful Moments:** If a conflict arises, use a silent grounding technique—like counting to three or noticing your breath—to remain steady.

By balancing your inner calm with empathy, you forge stronger connections without sacrificing your own stability.

Embracing Ongoing Self-Reflection
Even after you have made lots of progress, keep time in your routine for reflection:

- **Weekly or Monthly Check-Ins:** Ask yourself, "Am I slipping back into needing constant attention? Have I avoided listening to others' feelings?"
- **Self-Inquiry Questions:** "Have I respected my boundaries and others' boundaries this week? Did I show unnecessary harshness or react strongly to mild feedback?"
- **Adjust Plans if Needed:** If you notice slip-ups, decide on concrete ways to address them—such as returning to a daily breathing exercise you dropped.

Helping Others Grow

With your new insights, you can also support friends, family, or coworkers who might struggle with similar self-focused patterns or emotional challenges:

- **Lead by Example:** Show calmness, empathy, and respect in your interactions. Others may learn more from seeing these qualities in action than from being told.
- **Offer Resources:** If someone is curious about changing but does not know how, share relevant books or simple methods you have learned.
- **Avoid Forcing Change:** You cannot push someone else to change faster than they are ready. Gentle support is often more effective than demands.

Setting Challenges to Grow Further

To keep growing, you might create small challenges for yourself:

- **Plan an Empathy Day:** Make it a personal challenge to ask thoughtful questions to each person you speak with. Note how they respond.
- **Expand Your Circle of Concern:** Talk to someone you usually overlook, like a neighbor or a coworker from a different team. Practice curiosity and kindness.
- **Experiment with Acts of Service:** Offer help in a setting you have not tried before, such as volunteering or assisting an acquaintance with a project.

These challenges push you beyond your comfort zone, reinforcing that your changes are ongoing and alive.

Keeping Track of Stress Levels

High stress can tempt anyone to revert to self-protective or self-centered actions. Monitor your stress:

- **Plan Downtime:** Ensure each day or week has moments for rest or a calming activity.
- **Ask for Help When Overloaded:** If tasks pile up, see if you can delegate or lighten your load.
- **Maintain Healthy Sleep and Eating Patterns:** These basics keep your mood stable, making it easier to continue positive behaviors.

By managing stress, you protect yourself from being pushed into old habits under pressure.

Anticipating Changing Life Stages

Your needs and triggers can shift as life changes—new jobs, family events, health shifts, aging parents, or a move to a different area. Long-term positive change means you are ready to adapt:

- **Review Old Tools:** If your previous approach to stress management stops working in a new environment, explore new methods.
- **Stay Curious:** Each life stage might bring fresh insights into empathy and self-awareness.
- **Reconnect with Support Networks:** Whenever big changes occur, ensure you have the help you need—friends, mentors, or counselors.

Transforming Hurdles into Lessons

Even in a positive, empathetic life, challenges will arise—conflicts, misunderstandings, personal disappointments. Use them as lessons:

- **Conflict:** Practice calm listening and boundary setting. Each conflict resolved kindly strengthens your skills.
- **Misunderstandings:** Check how you communicate. Did you assume the other person's viewpoint? Or did you fail to explain your own?
- **Personal Disappointments:** Reflect on what you can learn, such as improving time management or being more realistic about outcomes.

By viewing obstacles as growth opportunities, you remain on the path of change rather than seeing them as proof you should revert to old habits.

Passing On the Values

If you have children or younger relatives, you can guide them to adopt empathy, balanced thinking, and respectful boundaries from an early age. Even if you do not have children, you might mentor younger colleagues or be a supportive figure in your community:

- **Model the Behaviors Daily:** Children and younger people often imitate what they see.
- **Explain the Reasons:** When they ask why you handle conflicts calmly or respect others' feelings, share the simple logic behind it.
- **Encourage Them to Care About Others:** Simple tasks like having them check on a neighbor or help a sibling can build their habit of empathy.

Achievements of Others

Moving away from harmful self-focus also means noticing and honoring what others achieve. Clap for their success, ask them questions about how they got there, and express genuine interest:

- **Give Credit Publicly:** In group settings, if someone contributed to a project, acknowledge their part.
- **Offer Simple Praise:** "You did great on that assignment!" or "I appreciate your help on this."
- **Avoid Making Their Achievement About You:** Resist the urge to say, "That reminds me of when I..." Keep the spotlight on them.

Dealing with People Who Stay the Same

While you grow, not everyone in your circle will join you. Some may remain self-centered or even try to pull you back:

- **Show Consistent Kindness:** You can still treat them with respect while maintaining your own growth.
- **Use Boundaries When Needed:** If they violate your limits or refuse to respect changes you make, you can limit your exposure to their negativity.
- **Accept They May Not Change:** Their choices are theirs. Focus on what you can control—your actions, your attitude, your environment.

Reflecting on Your Inner Changes

A key sign of real progress is noticing how you feel inside compared to before:

- **Less Urge for Attention:** Maybe you find you do not need to be the center of every conversation.
- **Greater Calm in Stressful Moments:** Where you used to react with anger or panic, now you respond with a calmer mind.
- **More Interest in Others:** You might naturally ask how friends and coworkers are doing and truly care about their answers.

Observing these inner shifts can motivate you to keep going.

This entire path of change is not about reaching a final perfect state. It is about daily practice, growing stronger in empathy, and keeping a stable core. Honor how far you have come, remembering that each small step matters.

Maintaining Gratitude

Gratitude is a powerful tool for sustaining positive change. When you notice the good things—like a supportive friend, a small success, or a moment of calm in a hectic day—you shift your mindset away from negativity or self-obsession.

- **Daily Gratitude Check:** List one or two things you feel thankful for before sleeping.
- **Thank People Often:** A heartfelt thank-you to someone who helped you or brightened your day reinforces connections.
- **Look for Tiny Bright Spots:** Even on tough days, you might appreciate having a roof over your head or a skill you have improved.

Being Patient with the Pace

Sometimes, you might wish you could transform everything overnight. But lasting change is slow and steady. If you compare yourself to a version of perfection, you might feel discouraged. Instead, look back at how far you have already come.

- **Notice Old vs. New Behavior:** Think about a situation that once triggered a strong reaction. Are you handling it better now? That is progress.
- **Focus on Long-Term Gains:** The goal is a lifetime of healthier habits, not a quick fix.
- **Remain Flexible:** If one method stops working, try another. The main idea is to keep moving forward in caring and balanced ways.

Managing Expectations from Others

Friends and family who knew you as more self-focused might not believe your changes at first. They could still expect you to act in the old ways. Give them time:

- **Let Actions Speak:** Consistency over weeks and months will show them the difference.
- **Stay Calm if They Doubt You:** If they say, "You will never change," answer politely that you understand their doubt, but you are committed to improving.

Exploring New Opportunities

As you maintain empathy and calmness, new avenues might open up:

- **Leadership Roles:** People may see you as more reliable and caring, leading to greater responsibilities at work or in the community.
- **Deepened Friendships:** Old acquaintances might trust you more, since you are less centered on yourself and more on mutual support.
- **Personal Growth:** You might find the confidence to try new hobbies or training because you trust yourself to handle mistakes better.

Facing the Future with Steadiness
Life's twists and turns will keep coming. But with a balanced mind, a caring heart, and an understanding that healing is always a choice, you stand on firmer ground. You can greet new challenges with a calm curiosity: "What can I learn here?" instead of fearing them as threats to your worth.

Conclusion
Long-term positive change is an ongoing process, built on everything you have practiced: recognizing and reducing harmful self-focus, showing empathy, finding inner calm, respecting boundaries, and mending emotional wounds. Each of these skills weaves into a whole that supports kinder, more stable living.

By continuing to reflect, learn from setbacks, and remain open to growth, you sustain these changes through different stages of life. You become someone who sees others not as tools for your own needs but as people with feelings and needs of their own. You also become someone who can face stress and emotional challenges with a sense of balance rather than panic or ego.

While this book ends here, your personal growth does not. The steps you have taken and the lessons you have explored can keep guiding you in everyday life. Keep asking yourself how you can show kindness, keep a calm mind, and treat others with respect. In doing so, you reinforce a healthier vision of who you are and how you want to live—free from the chains of self-centered thinking and open to genuine connection with the world around you.

www.ingramcontent.com/pod-product-compliance
Lightning Source LLC
LaVergne TN
LVHW012107070526
838202LV00056B/5658